QE2 - A Ship For All Seasons

Foreword

by **Captain Robin A. Woodall RD★**, RNR Retd, HCMM, FJMU (Captain [Retired] RMS *Queen Elizabeth 2*)

It had always been my ambition to go to sea. As a small boy living in London during the Second World War I used to enjoy looking at books of the sea, especially at those that included the great liners of that era, and thinking: "That is what I want to do - go to sea in those ships". I little thought then that one day I would fulfil that ambition. I have been very fortunate in realising this small boys dream and have served in many of Cunards famous passenger ships, including *Queen Elizabeth 2* for fourteen years of my forty-four years at sea, and feel very honoured to have been given command of that great ship from 1987 up to my retirement in 1994. So it gives me great pleasure to have been asked to write the Foreword for this updated and revised edition of "QE2 - A Ship For All Seasons".

The author is a great "Cunardphile" and has written many excellent books on various ships of the Cunard Line and this new edition of his book on QE2 is no exception. A fine "potted history" - warts and all! - of what is arguably the greatest ship in the world. Now thirty-five years on from the laying of her keel, this book catalogues her career right from her conception and through her many and varied changes. It also shows that she has always had the aim of pleasing her passengers - be it in peace or war.

Long may it continue, and I look forward to a third edition of this book in the years to come as her remarkable history is by no means over!

Captain Robin Woodall   Hoylake, Merseyside

Introduction

Like a regal matron that, in elegantly accepting the ageing process that comes to us all in bidding farewell to the slim, sleek looks of our youth, so the *Queen Elizabeth 2* has entered the fourth decade of her career having matured with an ease and grace that belies her years. Conceived with the future in mind by men of vision who swam against the tide of traditional thinking in ship design, the QE2 was soundly built to be versatile.

Achieving her destiny admirably, this great liner has now caught up with the future that had been anticipated for her (and thickening about her waist in the process!) and she has been extensively refitted to enable her to compete with much younger ships for years to come. Whether plying the vigorous waters of the North Atlantic between the Old and New Worlds in the summer season or sailing to exotic ports in the winter, the *Queen Elizabeth 2* is, indeed, "A Ship For All Seasons".

Widely regarded today as the most famous ship sailing in the world, the *QE2* creates enormous interest wherever she goes and in whatever she does. So popular is this ship that a huge new Cunarder is being planned to emulate her success on the Atlantic run.

The purpose of the updated edition of this book - as with its predecessor - is to provide an historical background - whilst including some of the events that have befallen her - as to why and how the QE2 was built; how she has adapted to change; what she has achieved; - and what she has survived!

Enjoy the book - enjoy the ship.

David F. Hutchings   Lee-on-The Solent, Hampshire

Dedication

To the memories of my parents whose love of the ships both great and small that passed through the waters of The Solent proved too infectious for me to resist.

Inside front cover: QE2 receives a salute from Concorde.R. Bruce Grice

Published by

Waterfront

A Division of Kingfisher Productions
**The Dalesmade Centre, Watershed Mill, Settle,
North Yorkshire BD24 9LR   Tel & Fax 0870 747 2983**
Copyright David F. Hutchings and Kingfisher Productions 2002
First Edition 1988, reprinted 1991,1993 and 2002
Printed by The Amadeus Press, Cleckheaton, West Yorkshire

Contents

Chapter One

A Ship for All Seasons

Cunard's mighty *Queen* liners were growing old.
From the years preceding the Second World War the *Queen Mary* – and the *Queen Elizabeth* since – had plied the North Atlantic between Europe and North America with a regularity and luxury that had brought full passenger lists and huge profits to the Cunard Steamship Company.

That is until 1957. In that year the numbers of passengers travelling by sea began to dwindle, the new jet airliners cutting the transatlantic journey from a crossing of four days by ship to just a few hours by air. That particularly fateful year proved to be the fulcrum of the fortunes of many shipping companies as the proportion of passengers being carried by air and sea reached 'evens'. From then on the scale of numbers being carried weighed heavily in favour of the airlines. Over the next decade many ocean liner companies would cease to exist as profits and passengers (especially the tourist and businessman) took to the air, preferring the quicker, time and money-saving passage that came with the aircraft, flying above the bad weather of winter.

Cunard had anticipated that they would eventually have to replace their two beloved *Queen* superliners (these had been the realisation of a long cherished dream to operate a weekly trans-

atlantic service with just two express liners). Accordingly, by the late 'fifties, the line had drawn plans for replacements, but the planned ships would be on a 'like-for-like' basis, albeit built with updated technology. Within the company's board of directors there was a hard-core of traditionalists who believed that the aircraft presented no more than a temporary setback to the institution that was Cunard: passengers would always prefer to travel by sea!

The proposed ships would continue the usual North Atlantic trade and be designed purely for the route. No consideration was entertained that the ships might go cruising during the unprofitable winter months when the prospect of a rough crossing on the notoriously wintery Atlantic, the roughest ocean in the world at that time of year, deterred many a prospective traveller. As passengers sometimes struggled to maintain a footing 'Getting there is half the fun!', Cunard's famous slogan, ceased to have much meaning at that time of year.

By 1959 the designs were advanced far enough for Cunard to approach the Government for financial assistance to enable the company to proceed with their new project. As before with the *Queen Mary* and *Queen Elizabeth* a loan was to be sought which

Leaving Southampton's Ocean Terminal is the magnificent *Queen Elizabeth*. This prima donna of the Atlantic gave her name to the 'New Cunarder'.
Southampton City Museums

Right: Sir John Brocklebank, chairman of Cunard, shakes hands with Sir Matthew Slattery, chairman of BOAC, after signing the BOAC-Cunard agreement on 6th June 1962. Sir Basil Smallpeice (right) was at the time, managing director of BOAC, little realising his future intimate involvement with Cunard.   *British Airways*

Above: A VC10 at London Airport (now Heathrow) proudly shows off its new BOAC-Cunard logo. The lettering of each company's name seems to be in proportion to the number of shares held by each!

British Airways

would similarly be fully repaid, thus making the new ships unique amongst their peers of other nations in being self-sufficient in their operation rather than being subsidised.

The Government, in its turn, formed a committee in September 1959 led by Lord Chandos to consider Cunard's application. After due investigation, two 75,000 ton ships were recommended with speeds of 30 knots and carrying 2,270 passengers.

Soon after the Chandos Committee was formed Cunard's chairman, Colonel Denis Bates, died and Sir John Brocklebank was appointed as his successor.

During the early years of his chairmanship Sir John resurrected an idea that had originally been formulated in the early 'thirties by the then chairman, Sir Percy Bates, to put Cunard into the air business. Subsequently, in 1959, Cunard bought Eagle Airways. In 1960 Cunard – Eagle, as the line would be known, applied for a licence to fly the Atlantic to New York and at the same time purchased two Boeing aircraft to show their determination. The licence was granted, then revoked after an appeal by BOAC.

Although Cunard carried on its air operations from the United Kingdom to Bermuda (and from there to New York etc)

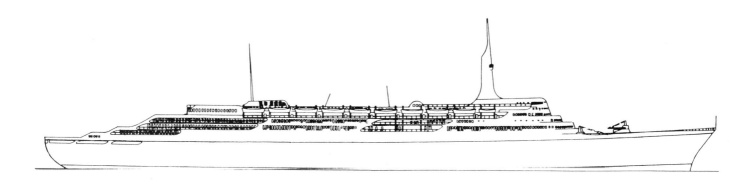

A drawing of 31st March 1961 shows a proposal for the Q3 project. The funnel configuration has not yet been decided but one could assume that it might have been similar to the John Brown-built Swedish liner *Kungsholm* that was launched in 1965.

Based on a drawing supplied by Liverpool University

the company finally came to an arrangement with BOAC in June 1962 and BOAC–Cunard was formed, with the shipping company holding a 30 per cent interest.

Perhaps the Government seeing Cunard spend £8.5 million on this new enterprise had second thoughts as the Chandos Committee now recommended that the company should be granted a loan for the building of only one new ship, designated 'Q3', and that she should be designed solely as a three class North Atlantic express liner. A loan of £17 million, at a low rate of interest, would be made available against the £28 million (maximum) that the new ship would be expected to cost. Many of the younger directors were still unhappy about the type of ship that was being selected and they found an ally in Sir John Brocklebank.

Sir John reappraised the whole situation – dwindling passenger numbers, increasing losses, potential actual cost of the Q3 by the time of building – and took a momentous decision and cancelled the new liner. He later described the decision to build her as a 'disaster'.

A fresh look was taken at the company's requirements and at the advances that had been made in the arts and technologies of shipbuilding, in propulsion machinery and in materials available to the shipbuilder. The new ship, Sir John Brocklebank stated, would not be an updated version of the two existing *Queens* nor would it be a re-working of the Q3 idea.

Sir John liked to refer to the new project as 'The New Cunarder' but the ship soon became known as the 'Q4'. Spike Milligan, that most zany of British comics, parodied the nomenclature theme for a television comedy series – 'Q6'. Other 'Qs' in this popular series followed thereafter.

The initial concept for 'The New Cunarder' was for the 27 and 12 boilers of the *Queen Mary* and *Queen Elizabeth* respectively, and their four propellers each, to be replaced in the Q4 by four boilers and two propellers. Modern engines etc had enabled an almost equal amount of power to be obtained from a smaller installation. Enough fuel would also be carried to last a complete round North Atlantic voyage at an average speed of 28.5 knots. 2,000 passengers, in three classes, would be carried in maximum safety with a corresponding reliability of service. Rooms, too, would be flexible in as much as they could be changed from one class to another, ideal for when cruising.

58,000 gross tons would be contained within the 960 foot hull and a beam of 104 feet would enable the liner to pass through the Panama and Suez Canals with just 18 inches clearance on either side of the former. This, with the ability to produce her own fresh water (the old *Queens* could carry enough only for a few days), would open up the world to the new ship.

The dual role of North Atlantic liner sailing and tropical ocean cruising became increasingly attractive to Cunard.

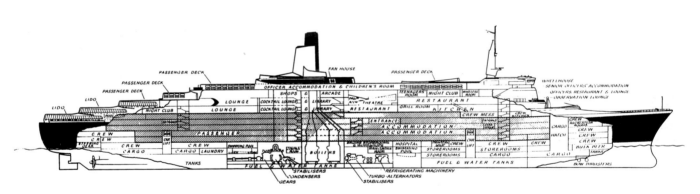

Q 4 — the new 58,000 ton CUNARDER

Advance publicity for No. 736 shows how the liner would be divided, although classes have not been designated.   *Cunard*

Chapter Two

Do or Die

Under the relatively short chairmanship of Sir John Brocklebank with his policy of 'new thinking', Cunard diversified its passenger operations.

Although Cunard was still carrying more passengers than any other shipping company, their transatlantic passenger service was developing into an ever increasing loss-maker and it was decided to send some of the other passenger ships in the fleet cruising. The only full-time cruise ship that Cunard operated was the luxurious *Caronia*, popularly known as 'The Dollar Princess' or 'The Green Goddess' because of the three shades of light green in which her hull was painted.

Cunard had also made a study of other Atlantic liners that had been sent cruising during the winter months as an alternative to running with that season's associated reductions in patronage on the northern ocean. The magnificent *France* of the French Line was studied in depth as was the US Lines' *United States*.

Ultimately two of the Cunard's Canadian service ships, *Saxonia* and *Ivernia*, were sent to John Brown's shipbuilding yard in Scotland for extensive rebuilding to convert them into cruise-ships. This was done in 1962, the liners reappearing as the *Carmania* and *Franconia*. The lessons learnt from this pair were of great practical benefit when the facilities and materials to be incorporated in the Q4 were being considered.

The experience in building a third sister, the *Sylvania*, of 1955 had also been of use. Plastic piping, plastic baths, lightweight furniture and specially developed, deeper than usual, girders (which had holes cut into them to enable easy passage of piping and electrical cables) had been used to facilitate the saving of weight and these ideas were to be used to advantage ten years later.

The *Mauretania* too went cruising and, then, in 1963 the mighty *Queens* found winter employment in this lucrative and expanding market. Their great prestige ensured that they were popular in their new roles, although their draughts of 38 feet and beams of 118 feet precluded their access to the harbours of many ports that they visited. Consequently they had to anchor offshore from these prohibited havens, ferrying passengers ashore by their own ship's boats.

It was planned that the Q4 should have a greatly reduced beam and draught in comparison to her predecessors: this was to be made possible by stringent weight saving through the careful use of lighter materials in her construction that had been made available from the very latest advances in technology. Thus the ports made inaccessible to her predecessors would be opened to the new ship, enabling her to moor alongside jetties in sheltered waters and allowing her passengers to disembark directly from ship to shore in comfort.

Cruising from New York, the *Elizabeth* sailed to the Bahamas and sometimes crossed the Atlantic to visit various ports in the Mediterranean. On this side of 'The Pond' the *Mary* sailed from Southampton, rolling her way through the Bay of Biscay with her stabilisers retracted (to conserve fuel en-route) to the Canaries, Lisbon and Gibraltar.

During one flying visit to the *Mary*, whilst she was calling at Cannes during 1966, Sir Basil Smallpeice paid a visit to his counterpart of the French Line who was on board the *France*, anchored a short way from the British ship. From this visit stemmed the idea of operating the 'Lizzie', and later the Q4, in mutual co-operation with the *France* instead of in competition. It was also planned that the *Mary* and *Elizabeth* should be kept in service until 1968 and 1969 respectively before withdrawing them. The 'Lizzie' would be kept on the route for a year longer than the *Mary* in order to provide the Q4 with a running mate. Commodore Geoffrey Marr was to keep the *Elizabeth* as his flagship with the captaincy of the Q4 passing to William ('Bil with one 'l' ') Warwick who would also stand by 'The New Cunarder' whilst she was being built.

But in 1966, because of its passenger fleet losses of the previous few years (only slightly alleviated in the early years of the decade by the more healthy revenue derived from the profits of its cargo operations before they, too, declined), Cunard's financial position deteriorated even further. This, combined with a £4 million loss caused by the lengthy seaman's strike of that year, forced the company to once more reappraise its position. An innovation for the company occurred with a switch to contain-erisation when Cunard joined, in December 1966, the Atlantic Container Line which saved the cargo business by its resultant profitability.

Sir Basil Smallpeice had by this time taken over the helm of the company and he proceeded to take the policy of Sir John Brocklebank's 'New thinking' to its brilliantly successful – albeit extremely unpopular at the time – conclusion. By re-thinking the new policies he arrived at the conclusion that ships should not merely be used as a means of getting from 'A' to 'B' but should be used as part of the journey, a hotel that took its passengers to places whilst, meanwhile, enjoying themselves during the passage.

Perhaps spurred on by shrewd observations from senior staff such as the fleet's newly appointed Commodore, Geoffrey Marr, who pointed out that the shore staff and offices had not

Carinthia and *Caronia* (The 'Green Goddess'), the last Cunard ships to go before 'Q4' came into service. *Norman Jackman*

The *Queen Mary*, the epitome of the ocean liner, leaves Southampton for a final cruise before her ultimate sailing on 31st October 1967 en-route to preservation and a whole new career in Long Beach, California.   *Southampton City Museums*

been trimmed to match the needs of the fleet and that in many instances posts and functions were excessively overmanned, Sir Basil put further economies into practice, convinced that to be a viable proposition the company had 'to do or die'.

Older ships and those not converted for cruising were sold (after the sale of the *Caronia* in May 1968 only the *Carmania* and *Franconia* were left); the main passenger office was moved from Liverpool to Southampton (March 1967); offices in many towns were shut and sold and Cunard's interest in BOAC – Cunard were bought back by BOAC, realising a handsome profit for the shipping company.

But the heaviest decision of all came as a blow to Britain generally: the beloved *Queens* were to be retired one year earlier than had been anticipated.

The *Mary* was withdrawn first on 20th September 1967. On board the old liner Captain John Treasure Jones, himself facing his own retirement, toasted a portrait of the 'New Cunarder' that was being launched in Scotland that day; on the 22nd the liner left New York for the last time after due honours had been paid to her by the city's Mayor, leaving behind a sadness and a void in the city that has never since been filled.

Everyone was losing 'their' *Queen*. As the three-funnelled Atlantic liner headed towards home, and a continuation of her destiny, she passed the *Queen Elizabeth* for the last time just after midnight in mid-Atlantic on September 25th. The sister ships bade a poignant, final farewell to each other with their mighty whistles as their illuminated funnels flashed on and off.

The *Mary* had been sold for £1.25 million to the City of Long Beach and, after a final short cruise from Southampton, sailed for her new home on October 31st, via Cape Horn, where she was refurbished as the 'Hotel Queen Mary', being rebuilt in some areas as an attraction centre. Well looked-after, she is still there – a legacy of art deco and luxury from the days when the sea track was the only highway between Europe and the USA.

A different fate awaited the *Queen Elizabeth*, however. It had been intended to sail her in conjunction with the Q4 for at least a year after the latter ship's introduction into service but a combination of Cunard's financial circumstances exacerbated by the seamens' strike and the partnership between the *Queen* and the *France*, which could be carried over to the new ship, caused her premature demise.

Sold to a somewhat 'shady' American consortium she left Southampton in circumstances very different from the emotive but affectionate farewell given to the *Mary*: it seemed as if she was being banished, sailing almost furtively, in the early morning fog. It had been planned to keep her in Philadelphia but she languished for two years, gradually rotting, at Port Everglades near Fort Lauderdale in Florida. After this interlude of despair she was again offered for sale and found a buyer in C.Y. Tung of Hong Kong.

Sailing from Florida in August of 1970 she was renamed *Seawise University*, undergoing conversion to a cruising university in Hong Kong.

Before she even once sailed in her new role she caught fire in several places at once and, after blazing for several days, rolled over and died. As in the mid-60s Cunard had spent $4m converting her for cuising and installing fire prevention standards to US regulations it was considered that the cause of destruction had been sabotage. A sad ending to the world's finest and largest ship, a symbol of Britain's post war recovery in the days of austerity and rationing.

Throughout this financially and emotionally complex period with its cut-backs at sea and the closure, sale or transfer of shore offices the main aims of the stringent rationalisation were carefully nurtured until they reached fruition with the survival of Cunard and the tangible result of the 'new thinking' – the planning and building of the most versatile liner that the world had yet seen.

On 19th August 1964 the Cunard line invited five shipbuilders to tender for the construction of the 'New Cunarder' and by 30th November the bids had been returned. Within one month the final choice had been made and the contract to build Q4 was awarded to the John Brown shipyard of Clydebank (the former builders of the *Queen Mary* and *Queen Elizabeth*) as their tender of £25,427,000 was the best received.

Just after 3pm, on 30th December within the augustly solid surroundings of the Bank of England, Sir John Brocklebank (then still chairman of the steamship company) and Lord Aberconway, chairman of John Brown and Company (Clydebank) Limited, signed the contract.

The initial contract called for a twin screw ship of 28.5 knots (less speed would be required for cruising), with four boilers and catering for the American, as well as the traditional, demand for three classes. One boiler was dispensed with during a later cost-cutting exercise and, in order to cut down on kitchen logistics and to provide an easier operating environment for cruising (when the ship would become one class), the ship sensibly also became a two-class vessel. These changes were decided upon even whilst the ship was building, an early indication of the design's versatility.

Cunard, it seemed, was set fair on a course for recovery and all bade well for the future – once the ship was completed.

But there were still shoals ahead.

Within the solid walls of the Bank of England on 30th December 1964, Sir John Brocklebank (for Cunard) and Lord Aberconway (for John Brown, Clydebank) sign the building contract for Q4 - the 'New Cunarder'. *Cunard*

Chapter Three

Building for the Future

July 2nd 1965 dawned a beautiful, bright day over the expectant shipyard of John Brown and Company Limited.

The keel of No. 736, the shipyard's order-book number for the 'New Cunarder', was due to be laid on the short length of wooden blocks that would eventually be extended down to the water's edge along the length of No. 4 slipway, the birthplace of many a Cunard ship, including the two mighty *Queens*. She was to be Cunard's 172nd ship and her keel laying was to take place just two days before the 125th anniversary of the company's founding by Samuel Cunard of Halifax, Nova Scotia.

From this neat row of blocks extended six baulks of timber placed horizontally at right angles to, and erected level with, the top of the blocks. To one side of the building blocks a prefabricated section of the new ship's keel and double bottom rested on these baulks and other temporary blocks waiting to be ceremoniously slid into place.

John Rannie, the managing director of the shipyard whose crowning achievement the Q4 would be (he would be retiring when the ship was finally handed over to Cunard), had stipulated that the prefabricated section being built in the workshops should weigh forty tons. This would be within the combined lifting capabilities of two tower cranes adjoining the slip which, with the aid of a powerful winch fixed to the concrete base of a long vanished derrick crane, would lift and pull the keel section into place.

At least, that was the plan.

Lady Aberconway, the wife of John Brown's chairman, had agreed to perform the ceremony and various reporters had been invited along to witness the occasion. At the appointed time the cranes took the strain of the steel section and the winch commenced to take in the slack on the wire cables. Unfortunately the cranes were designed to lift their maximum load of 20 tons each in a vertical direction and not at the angle induced by the pull on the winch.

After moving slightly the keel section refused to move any further which placed an enormous strain on the winch. Consequently, as the winch continued to pull in its cable, the entire concrete block into which it was fixed started a process of being extracted from the earth, dried out during recent fine weather.

The ceremony thus came to a hasty and slightly undignified halt and the pressmen were quickly ushered into the Model Room where they were liberally entertained.

The recalcitrant keel section was quietly eased into position onto the building blocks on the following Monday, 5th July, by a carefully chosen gang of men who had delayed their start of the local 'Clydebank Fair'; the shipyard was normally closed-down during the fortnight of this annual holiday.

After an initial public embarrasment, the keel of No. 736 was quietly slid into place on Monday 5th July 1967.   *Boyd Haining*

Even before the contract had been signed an air of confidence that the company would be given the contract to build Q4 had existed within the boardroom of John Brown's. This confidence, almost mounting to an assumption, was based on the Company's record of building many previous famous Cunarders such as the *Lusitania*, *Aquitania* and, of course, the *Queen Mary* and *Queen Elizabeth*. The prevailing confidence even extended to the pronouncement of an early delivery date for the completed 'New Cunarder': one which would have unhappy consequences.

During the months preceding the laying of the first few symbolic tons of the new 736, a mass of work had already taken place. Calculations, drawings, estimates and planning, the preparation of network charts (showing in a numerical and time form what job had to be done, in which order and when – in

Many funnel designs were considered and tested at John Brown's. Here some of the designs are shown together.
University of Liverpool, Cunard Archives

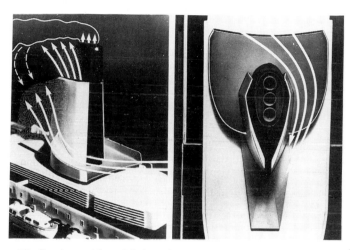

The liner's novel funnel design, shown here on a large model, with added arrows graphically showing the wind direction induced by the wind-scoop and casing. *University of Liverpool, Cunard Archives*

order to avoid 'bottlenecks' and hold-ups) had all been started. The advance ordering of much material had also gone ahead and the basic design principles had been established. These latter criteria would not be changed, whatever else was, and included positions of support pillars, bulkheads and, most importantly, the location of engines. This was determined as being just aft of amidships (for stability and strength): in turn this dictated funnel location which, being placed almost amidships, allowed the development of a dual purpose series of terraced decks, cascading down through five decks towards the stern, providing shelter during North Atlantic passages and offering delightful sun-traps whilst cruising.

Heading Cunard's design team were their naval architect, Dan Wallace, and technical director, marine engineer Tom Kameen. Dan Wallace had served his apprenticeship in the esteemed shipyard to which he now returned, finding himself senior to those who had once been his peers.

John Brown's own prestigious but secretive design office was led by the yard's technical director, John Stark, who also had responsibility for the yard's experimental tank in which were tested differing hull models of the new liner until one had been perfected. On the forefoot of the ship a 'bulb' would be fitted; this bulbous bow would 'punch a hole' in the water ahead of the ship thereby cutting down water resistance on the hull – and also cut down the fuel bills. The traditional bow wave, beloved of all marine artists, would disappear, robbing Q4 of her 'bone in the teeth' when she was underway.

Cunard's naval architect, Dan Wallace (right), discusses a point of the Q4's design. *University of Liverpool, Cunard Archives*

From the initial laying of the keel the erection of steelwork on No. 4 slip went on at a steady pace. Extra men were taken on when necessary and if they did not hold any documentary evidence that they were competent at their trade then they were given a test task.

To maintain an adequate supply of steel sections (such as angle-bar and tee-bar) the steel mills in the vicinity of Clydebank would give advance notice of their rolling dates of particular sections to the drawing office so that sufficient time could be allowed for ordering. Weekly co-ordinating visits by John Brown's commercial manager to the mills also ensured that a flow of information was maintained.

Aluminium alloy was to be used in great quantities in the construction of the superstructure once the steel hull had been completed. 1,100 tons, the largest amount (including some of the biggest plates) ever used on a British liner, were to be supplied by Alcan who organised a special training centre within the yard. The trained welders were also periodically checked for standards of workmanship which thus remained high throughout the building of the ship.

Above: Several differing models of the Q4's hull were built and tested in John Brown's towing tank. One model is shown being put through its paces in simulated rough weather conditions.
University of Liverpool, Cunard Archives.

Left: 1,100 tons of aluminium was to be used in the liner's superstructure and much of it was prefabricated in the shipyard's workshops.
University of Liverpool, Cunard Archives

A workshop for the preparation of the aluminium plates (of which many were delivered in ready-to-use sizes) was specially dedicated for this purpose having its floor treated with a special sealant to prevent any foreign particles affecting the metal. As soon as the aluminium was prepared and welded into prefabricated units it was primed with a special anti-corrosion paint and this remained superbly effective throughout construction.

The use of aluminium (along with other innovative weight saving design features) had enabled the design team to reduce the liner's draught by several feet than if steel had been used in the superstructure. It also enabled the number of decks to be increased from 12 in the old *Queens* to 13 in the Q4.

The addition of an extra passenger deck more than compensated for the limits on length and beam that had been imposed by the planned usage of the Panama and Suez Canals. This additional deck had also been made possible by the reduction of 6 to 9 inches in the heights of other decks by running electrical cables, piping and ventilation trunking over main passageways and bathrooms where a lower headroom was acceptable. Cunard's engineering staff had also managed to save a creditable 3 feet in the height of the machinery spaces.

Lloyd's ship surveyors were also keenly interested in the superstructure as it was to be regarded as part of the ship's strength structure. Accordingly, expansion joints (the narrow, protected transverse 'gaps' in the uppermost deck of a ship that allowed the superstructure to 'work' in heavy weather when the main hull bends) were omitted.

To prevent any corrosive electrolytic interaction between the steel of the hull and the aluminium superstructure a careful bonding method had to be utilised. A special epoxy compound was spread along the joints between the two metals and then steel rivets were used for the final connection.

Left: Surrounded by a web of scaffolding, the curved stem and bulbous bow already display their elegant curves.　　　*Boyd Haining*

Below: Partially built from prefabricated sections, these deck houses on the boat deck will soon accommodate the Double Up Room, shops and theatre balcony.　　　*University of Liverpool, Cunard Archives*

The various weight saving exercises proved to be a worthwhile – and potentially profitable – operation but it also affected the centre of gravity which, as a consequence, had to be lowered. The usual method of remedying this problem would have been to add, in the Q4's case, 750 tons of otherwise useless ballast to the bottom of the ship. But the designers ingeniously did away with the use of this dead weight and instead turned it to advantage.

Their solution was to increase certain steel plate thicknesses in areas where greater than usual wear (or corrosion) could be reasonably expected to occur, such as in the lower most structure in way of machinery and the fore part of hull, strengthening it against ice. Increasing the weight of steel work within the double bottom by constructing more closely subdivided double bottom cells also added to the ship's strength.

Of the many thousands of items that were to be fitted into the hull of No. 736, many had to be made specially for the liner.

The propulsion machinery – boilers, turbines, gearboxes, condensers and propeller shafts – and much ancilliary machinery was made by John Brown Engineering (Clydebank) Limited but built under licences from the respective designers or developers. Much of the machinery had been conceived in its original form in the years succeeding 1954 when the idea of replacements for the *Mary* and *Elizabeth* were first mooted, culminating in the ill-fated Q3 project. The Q3 designs were resurrected and modified until the machinery for the Q4 was finally chosen. Reliability, simplicity and efficiency were to be the watchwords.

Twenty seven boilers in the *Queen Mary* and twelve in the *Queen Elizabeth* had given 160,000 shaft horse power to four propellers (40,000 shp each) to give a service speed of 28.5 knots.

Left: With launching cradle in place and with new paint gleaming, the bow of the 'Q4' towers above the slipway.
University of Liverpool, Cunard Archives

Below: One of the two 19-foot six-bladed propellers, each weighing 31 tons 13 cwt (32,157 hg), poised above the tidal Clyde. Each of these propellers would absorb 55,000 shp to give a service speed the same as the old Cunard *Queens*.   *University of Liverpool, Cunard Archives*

Advances in marine engineering had been such that the Q4 was to have four watertube boilers which would deliver 120,000 shp giving the same speed from only two propellers. The propeller manufacturers, Stone Manganese Marine of Greenwich, were concerned at the amount of power that each of their products would have to absorb and were greatly relieved when, because of economies, the four boilers were reduced to three. 110,000 shp would now be produced, giving the same service speed.

The boilers were of Foster Wheeler ESD II design and, at 278 tons each, were the largest ever constructed for a marine installation. Steam was produced at 850 pounds per square inch at a temperature of 950°F (later rising to 1,000°F).

The steam was fed into two sets of turbines (double reduction, double helical, dual tandem gearing) which were built to a design by Pametrada Limited. Pametrada or, to give its proper title, Parsons Marine Engineering Turbine Research and Development Association (supported by shipbuilding and various marine turbine engineering firms) was the successor to the firm founded by the inventor of the turbine, Sir Charles Parsons.

The magazine 'Engineering' described the turbines: 'Each set is a two-cylinder unit, in which the flow from the high-pressure turbine feeds one double-flow low-pressure turbine, exhausting into an underslung condenser. The turbines are connected to the main shaft by a dual tandem arrangement of double helical gears'.

Amongst many companies that produced other machinery for various purposes AEI built three turbine-generators which would produce the ship's life forces, steam and electricity, for the various ship's services. Many years later AEI, as part of the GEC group, would have a further major involvement in the life of the liner.

However, to ensure that the maximum, most efficient use was obtained from the available machinery space, a scale model was made showing the positions of every pipe and piece of gear.

The 'New Cunarder', like her predecessors before her, loomed over her surroundings during her building. Because she was practically all-welded the traditional sounds of rivetting no longer sent their staccato rhythms out over Clydebank.

There was a quietness in the town, a silent overture to the coming years of change.

One of the many items contracted-out to smaller firms. Here one of the propeller cones is about to leave Southampton-based Hardingham Pressure Vessels Ltd. for Glasgow.
Roger Hardingham

Two sets of stabilisers were built into No. 736 enabling, amongst other things, the restaurants to be carried higher in the ship.
Boyd Haining

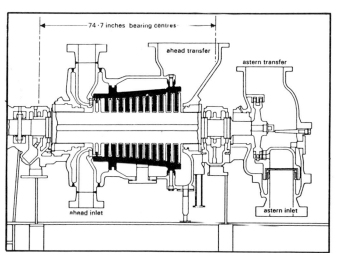

Diagram showing the high pressure ahead turbine and astern turbine. Because of the high temperatures involved, stainless iron blades were used.
Engineering Magazine

Chapter Four

Fourteen to One

Yard No. 736 rested sleek and serene on the stocks of Slip Number 4.

Her Majesty, Queen Elizabeth II, had graciously consented to launch the new liner and for many weeks previous to the chosen day a great deal of conjecture surrounded the possible name of the new ship.

Many suggestions had been put forward: *Princess Anne, Queen of Britain, British Queen, Queen Victoria* (a name previously mooted for the subsequently named *Queen Mary*), *Britannia* (Cunard's first ship), *Prince Charles, New Britain, John F. Kennedy* and *Churchill* were amongst the more serious contenders that found varying odds in the betting shops.

Perhaps it was because one *Queen Elizabeth* was still in service that that particular name did not attract much attention for the new ship. Odds of 14 to 1 were offered. Her Majesty's own name (although Queen Elizabeth II of England she was yet Queen Elizabeth I of Scotland) did not figure high in the betting stakes.

Even at this eleventh hour before the launch there had been anxious moments in the higher echelons of Cunard. A loss of £3.5 million had just been announced on the passenger ship operations and, to aggravate matters even more, an increase in the cost of Q4 was expected to be in the region of £4 million. (A final price of £29,091,000 would eventually be agreed in later months).

The £17.6 million loan that the company had secured from the Government was clearly not going to be enough, so Sir Basil Smallpeice met Sir Harold Lever, Financial Secretary to the Treasury, on September 13th, just one week before the launch date.

The result announced on the 14th was an increase of the original loan to £24 million and the day was saved. The £24 million was later reduced by £4 million when Cunard found that the full amount was not eventually needed. This was because the sales of the *Carinthia, Sylvania, Queen Elizabeth* and *Caronia* in 1968 realised £7 million. This would leave, other than Q4, only two ships in service, the *Carmania* and *Franconia*, and the three ships would be marketed by the newly-formed Cunard Line Limited.

So, not only did Cunard still have a business that they were once in danger of losing but they had a new ship and a new hope for the future, all won by so much drastic economic surgery of ships and men.

Q4 almost ready for launching as seen from the Clyde.

Steam and Sail

Her Majesty The Queen, HRH Prince Philip, The Duke of Edinburgh, and John Brown's Shipyard Director, George Parker, pause during a tour of the ship prior to the launching of No. 736. Sir Basil Smallpeice, Chairman of Cunard, stands to the left.

University of Liverpool, Cunard Archives

The mood of a revived Cunard seemed to be reflected by the sunshine that greeted the Queen on her arrival at Clydebank on 20th September 1967.

The launch of the 'New Cunarder', like the launches of her illustrious predecessors, had occupied the talk of the people of the upper reaches of the Clyde for many a day, and thousands flocked to the yard or to the fields on the opposite side of the Clyde, to view the proceedings.

The weather was made ideal by a light westerly wind which helped to ensure that the required depth of water would be available at the end of the standing ways in good time for the launch. Wind of another 5 knots would have presented a problem, however.

Stewards were posted at various points within the viewing compounds and at various danger points such as at cranes where individuals could be deterred from climbing them to obtain a better view.

Princess Margaret (she had previously opened an exhibition of the Q4's specially designed fitments at the Design Centre) had arrived in Glasgow on the eve of the launch, touring the launch slipway the following day. Her early appearance increased the odds on the selection of her name for the liner.

John Brown's managing director, John Rannie, greeted the Queen on her arrival, outshining Sir Basil Smallpeice and his own chairman, Lord Aberconway, as her host. After introducing Her Majesty to various leading figures involved with Q4, John Rannie accompanied the Queen on her tour to inspect the launching trigger which she would soon be remotely activating.

The launching party then ascended to the platform at the very bow of the ship, against which the bottle of champagne would shortly be splitting and frothing.

Continuing the traditions of the launching ceremony the Queen was handed an envelope containing a sheet of paper on which was written the long-kept secret − the proposed name of the new liner. (The written reminder of the ship's name had become a considered necessity ever since an august personage had forgotten the name of the ship to be launched!) A similar envelope had been deposited in the safe at Cunard's New York office, just in case of a breakdown in communications. Her Majesty refused the proferred envelope. 'I won't be needing that!' she joked, then spoke clearly into the microphones: 'I name this ship *Queen Elizabeth the Second*. May God bless her and all who sail in her'. It was 2:28pm.

A great roar went up from several thousand throats as the Queen cut the ribbon, using the same gold scissors that her mother and grandmother had previously used in the performance of launching their Royal namesakes, releasing the christening wine that stiffly swung its way to destruction. A button was then pressed that electrically released the launching trigger that kept a last land-locked hold on the mighty hull.

The Queen, the first reigning British monarch to launch a liner, had used her intuition to name the ship. The envelope that she had refused − and the one in New York − had contained the name *Queen Elizabeth*.

After the launch Sir Basil Smallpeice consulted with the Queen's Private Secretary Sir (later Lord) Michael Adeane and it was decided that the suffix 'Second' would be written as the Arabic '2', and not as the Roman 'II'.

This was done for several reasons. Firstly, it was good publicity; secondly, only battleships had carried a reigning monarch's Romanic suffix, thirdly, the ship was to be the second ship to bear the name *Queen Elizabeth*, a nice deference to both the Queen and the Queen Mother after whom the first *Lizzie* had been named as Queen Consort; and, fourthly – and perhaps most importantly – the Queen was still, in fact, only Queen Elizabeth I of Scotland and to name the ship with 'II' would have been an insult to the people of the country that had now produced a fitting successor to the Queens *Mary* and *Elizabeth*.

As the last wedges retaining the ship on the slip were knocked away, the ship seemed to stick on the well-greased standing ways and only to the trained eye did she apparently move. A voice shouted, 'Give her a push!' and George Parker, the shipyard director, stepped forward and jokingly did so! Slowly at first, then with an ever increasing momentum, the QE2 slid over tons of tallow towards her fast-approaching element.

Bundles of drag chains, weighing hundreds of tons in total (which had lain neatly alongside the launching ways, attached to the hull cables and later-to-be-removed eye bolts) gradually moved into rattling, clanking motion as the ship pulled them with her towards the specially-dredged River Clyde. The purpose of these bundles was to slow the ship down as she entered the water on this the first, short – but most dangerous – journey of her life, and to prevent her ramming the opposite bank of the river with her stern.

As the new *Queen* touched the water a perfectly timed anchor-formation of aircraft from the appropriately designated No. 736 Squadron of the Fleet Air Arm flew overhead.

The many hundreds of people in the fields opposite the shipyard had been warned by the police that the expected mini-tidal wave generated by the liner's entry into the water would

Above: Just minutes before the launch. The Q4 stands proud and ready on No. 4 slipway.
University of Liverpool, Cunard Archives

Left: At 2.30 pm on 20th September 1967 No. 736 is launched by Her Majesty Queen Elizabeth II. The liner would now be known as *Queen Elizabeth 2*, the QE2. A crowd of thousands watch as the liner takes to the water for the first time.
University of Liverpool, Cunard Archives.

Nearing completion, the liner is freshly painted and almost ready for launching.   *Boyd Haining*

A trip to the fields on the opposite side of the Clyde to the shipyard always proved a worthwhile journey. Shipbuilding and agriculture are indelibly intertwined in this evocative photograph.   *Boyd Haining*

From the opposite bank of the Clyde the *QE2* is seen to advantage as she makes contact with the water.
University of Liverpool, Cunard Archives.

probably flood the edge of the fields in which they stood. But once the launch was over the crowd moved forward to watch the 'New Cunarder', the *QE2*, as she was taken into care by tugs. Ushered towards the fitting-out jetty which would be her home for several months to follow, she would here take on the apparel appropriate for the world's newest *Queen*.

Meanwhile the official launch party headed towards the specially refurbished Mould Loft where a champagne afternoon tea had been arranged. A luncheon had been precluded because of the time of the launch and by the Royal party's programme.

Boyd Haining, then shipyard manager, remembers the tea as 'a delightful affair consisting of dainty sandwiches in variety, and gooey cakes and gateaux. Toasts were taken in champagne selected by Aberconway, knowing HM's taste. The champagne was a heady one – Krug Privee Curee, demi-sec, vintage 1961'.

In his chairman's post-launch speech Lord Aberconway voiced what would in effect be the beginning of the end of John Brown's shipyard as an independent entity. He said that the *QE2* would be the last ship of note of which it could be said 'she was a John Brown ship'. Economics were again at work.

He continued:
'We have announced, with our friends and neighbours on the upper Clyde, that we intend to merge our shipbuilding interests. Without question this would be to the advantage of shipbuilding on the Clyde, of continued employment on the river, and of the country's economy. But it does carry with it the consequence that there will pass from the scene of shipbuilding the name of John Brown, a name which (though I should not say it) is second to none in fame and repute. This yard will go on, playing a major part in a wider shipbuilding setting, and will contribute its skills and traditions to the new organisation of which it will be part. Many great ships will be built and fitted out at Clydebank in the years to come, to the same standards as in the last seventy 'John Brown' years; they will be worthy successors to the *Queen Mary*, the *Queen Elizabeth* and the *Queen Elizabeth the Second*.'

The Queen, in her speech, said:
'I particularly welcome the opportunity you have given me to launch this splendid successor to those two famous Cunarders *Queen Mary* and *Queen Elizabeth*. I suppose these two ships were better known and loved, both in peace and war, by all of us living in these islands, than any other merchantman in our history. I have always had a special affection for them because they were named after my grandmother and my mother, and it does not seem so very long ago that I was present with my sister when my mother launched the *Queen Elizabeth*.

Every great enterprise has an element of risk and uncertainty about it, and I am sure no-one can predict the future career of the new Cunarder. I am equally certain that, in the experienced and capable hands of the Cunard company, she will stand the best chance of a happy and profitable lifetime.'

The element of risk and uncertainty of which the Queen spoke would be realised sooner than any of those present could predict.

Of the proposed, and hopefully beneficial, amalgamation of the upper Clyde shipyards the Queen remarked:
'We have all read, with a touch of nostalgia, that the name of John Brown is to disappear from the list of great shipbuilders. However, this does not mean that the very special skill and spirit of this yard will be lost to Clydeside or to British shipbuilding. In wishing the *Queen Elizabeth the Second* a long life and good fortune on all her voyages, I add my best wishes for success and prosperity to the new consortium of Clydeside shipbuilders.'

Instead of the usual piece of jewellery the Queen was then presented with a new motor launch for the Royal Yacht *Britannia*. 'I suppose we ought to paint it in Cunard colours and call it *John Brown*!' said Her Majesty. 'Why not paint it brown and call it *Cunard*!' retorted a wit at the top table.'

Within a very short time, under the recommendations of the Geddes Committee, John Brown would become the Clydebank division of Upper Clyde Shipbuilders. It would be under the regime of this new consortium under the chairmanship of Tony Hepper but with John Rannie still in direct control of the *QE2* project, that the liner would be finished.

Chapter Five

The Element of Risk

The liner lay berthed alongside the fitting out jetty, her empty compartments soon to be transformed into carpeted rooms of luxury or hygienically tiled storerooms and kitchens.

But meanwhile she contained a bustle of men and machines. Cables lay like black snakes along the decks or hanging down from overhead and the shouts and calls of the skilled workforce filled the corridors, rooms and machinery spaces as they went about their myriad tasks.

Fitting, inspecting and testing carried on, day in, day out until, part by part, the *QE2* metamorphosed from what appeared to be chaos to the casual viewer, to a unity of practical beauty.

The *QE2* was to be a showpiece for Great Britain, for her country's art, design and engineering skills, not only now in the late 1960s but in the decades to follow. Her decor had not only to be modern but futuristic; it had to anticipate tastes for years to come – an almost impossible task for the designers involved.

But it was done.

In the past the interior decoration had almost been left to chance and a hotchpotch of styles were used that, as a whole, sometimes lacked unity.

Sometimes a chairman's wife might be given the task of choosing materials; in large ships renowned architects, more used to designing country mansions, were also appointed and the resultant decor in the ships' lounges and restaurants would reflect the lavish days of Imperial Rome, Classical Greece or elegant, timbered English mansions. The sea outside was almost deliberately forgotten.

The *Queen Mary* had perfectly reflected the art of the 1930s in her Art-Deco, architectural interiors (her 'Ocean Liner' style becoming more popularly known as 'Odeon') but these had soon dated. The *Queen Elizabeth* became the symbol of British post-war recovery and great things were done with the available materials. But she too, partially reflected pre-war design and was stylishly and architecturally luxurious.

Safely berthed alongside the fitting-out jetty, the *QE2* takes on the appareil of a luxury liner, still surrounded by the bustle of the shipyard.
Scottish Record Office

QE2 would be everything inside and out. She would reflect the art and technology of the 1960s whilst being timeless. She would also have a carefully built-in versatility rather than built-in architecture that would enable her to change to reflect new tastes and styles.

The style of the 'Swinging 1960s' that had made Britain the leader in world design and fashion, along with the bright, colour awareness which had been distilled and matured from the early 1960s, all helped to create the feel of the QE2. To ensure that the best in design was made available to Cunard the Council of Industrial Design was consulted.

Lady Brocklebank, wife of Cunard's chairman at the time when Q4's contract was signed, had originally been appointed to lead a team of designers. Her wide experience of travel, of ships and hotels ('I know what people like and dislike' she once said) made her admirably qualified for the post.

Lady Brocklebank disappeared from the scene upon the retirement through ill-health of her husband but not before she had appointed James Gardner as co-ordinator for the whole design.

James Gardner (he had designed the successful 'Britain Can Make It' exhibition at the end of the war) was 60 and had become a scholarship student at Chiswick School of Art at the age of 12! His remit was to balance the design of the ship and his main responsibility lay with the aesthetics of the liner's external appearance.

Because of Gardner's other work commitments, Dennis Lennon became joint co-ordinator and together they gave the QE2 a balance of design. Everything was to be attractive but practical. There would not be one 'gimmick' on the ship and the two men would work closely with Dan Wallace, Cunard's naval architect, whose own team designed the structural layout of the ship often considering the needs of the interior designers in their work. The design team came from Britain, Canada and Australia.

From the earliest days of the Q4's construction, highly detailed mock-ups of various cabins had been built in the shipyard and these were constantly visited by design team members and many changes were affected. Passengers preferred beds to bunks

Mr. James Gardner had overall responsibility for the 'New Cunarder's' interior design and exterior appearance.
Shipbuilding & Shipping Record

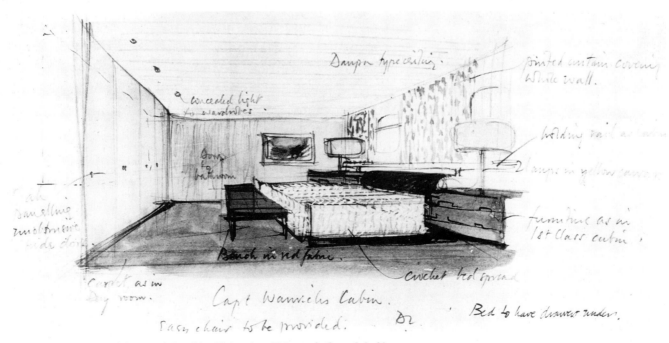

A designer's sketch of the captain's cabin. *University of Liverpool, Cunard Archives*

'Real' wood was used in several areas on the liner, such as in passenger furniture and decorative veneers and this photograph shows the Signal Deck being laid with teak planking.

Architectural Press

Fitting out alongside the jetty at John Brown's Clydebank shipyard. Here the funnel had already been fitted.

George Gardner

Above: A view of the Double Room, looking forward, from the top of the sweeping stainless steel and glass stairway. In later refits, amongst other changes, the upper lounge (the Double Up) would be given over as an extension of the shopping services.
University of Liverpool, Cunard Archives

Left: One of the majority of cabins that have a porthole. Compact and comfortable - luxury at sea available to everyone.
University of Liverpool, Cunard Archives.

Below: The space-age circular midships lobby. This would act as a lounge during voyages but would be the first class reception area whilst in harbour.
University of Liverpool, Cunard Archives

Part of the main kitchen on Quarter Deck as built. This kitchen would serve the Britannia Restaurant on the Upper Deck above it, the Columbia Restaurant aft on the same deck level as the kitchen and the Grill Room.   *University of Liverpool, Cunard Archives*

and a great proportion of the rooms (the word 'cabin' was dropped) were so fitted. Bath and showers were fitted more widely in rooms than ever before.

During the building of the liner it was decided   after much difference of opinion – that a two-class ship would be more advantageous than a three class vessel (especially for conversion to cruising when she would become, to all intents and purposes, a one class ship). The existence of the mock-up cabins ensured that no real difficulties occurred because of this change of direction. The opportunity to change to two classes arose when delays in the building occurred: Cunard turned these to their advantage. One major disadvantage of the delays was that the 1968 Summer season on the North Atlantic would be lost.

Extra space was also made available by the resultant reduction in the number of public rooms and associated services. By one brilliant stroke two lounges (tourist and cabin) on adjacent decks were made into one, two decks high, with the upper lounge providing a lounge balcony overlooking the lower. The two decks were connected with a stainless steel and glass stairway, cascading from one deck level to the next. This brilliant joining of the two lounges became the 20,000 square foot Double Room, one of the largest rooms afloat.

Two restaurants instead of three, and one kitchen to serve both, were to be raised from the traditional position of such rooms in earlier ships. The Verandah Grills in the earlier *Queens* had been popular, even in rough weather, because they were high in the ship and had large windows with sea-views. The other restaurants on the older ships were sited low down in the hull in order to reduce motion during stormy weather; (but they still remained un-patronised in such condition).

It was therefore decided to raise the restaurants in the *QE2* to the superstructure. The use of aluminium and the installation of stabilisers during building enabled the extra weight to be carried higher in the ship and both rooms were extended to the ship's side. Large windows built near to deck level gave wonderful views of the sea.

The kitchen, too, was raised for easy access to the restaurants, one aft and the other on the deck directly above the kitchen. Large windows were not needed in the kitchen so portholes were retained. One problem was noted by Jim Jone as he looked over the ship, as so many Cunard sea-going personnel did, to offer the benefit of his experience. In the *Mary* and the *Elizabeth* the kitchens, being low in those ships, had a garbage shute which opened to the sea through the bottom of the ship and down which rubbish could be jettisoned. There was no such shute on the *QE2* so garbage would have to be bagged and manually thrown overboard. That is, until a special door was cut into the side of the ship, disguised behind the large 'U' of the red CUNARD logo painted on the superstructure at the fore end of Quarter Deck.

One of the most elegant rooms afloat. Michael Inchbald's 'Queens Room' was decorated in white and silver and could be used for a variety of purposes.
Philip Rentell

Many of the layouts of public rooms and cabins had been created by the carefully selected group of designers with their designs co-ordinated by James Gardner and Dennis Lennon.

Some remarkably pleasant rooms were created and many designs were discarded along the way. Natural lighting was to be used as far as possible to take advantage of the large windows. The public rooms could be extended to the ship's side at night by utilizing what would be promenade space during the day.

As James Gardner was busy with the exterior styling of the ship Dennis Lennon carried on with some of the interior designs. Amongst his work were the Britannia Restaurant, the Queen's Grill (the successor to the popular Verandah Grills on the previous *Queen* liners where, on the payment of a supplement, passengers could enjoy an exclusivity denied to other passengers), the Theatre Bar (in shades of red) and the Midship's Bar (dark, mostly in greens).

The enormous Double Room (the balcony known as the Double Up, the lower deck the Double Down) was created by Jon Bannenberg and decorated with a red carpet and plum coloured suede walls. Bannenberg also did the Card Room in various greens and the swimming pool, on Six Deck, with its round changing rooms.

The classic Queen's Rooms, one of the most beautiful rooms ever to go to sea with its trumpet like columns, was finished in white and silver with a walnut veneered wall at one end which looked more substantial than suggested by its construction. A bust of the Queen, by Oscar Nemon, was set into a recess in this wall. Carpets and curtains gave a splash of colour in reds, honey

and lemon patterns. Its designer, Michael Inchbald, also designed the Quarter Deck library, furnished with chairs of green leather, brown tweed sofas and other chairs of black hide and brass.

Don Wallace, Cunard's naval architect, designed the Midships Lobby with its twenty-six foot diameter recess. This lobby with its dark blue leather walls, would act as a reception area in port and as a lounge whilst at sea. Curved green sofas bordered the recess.

The superb 500-seat theatre could also be used as a conference hall or as a church as well as a cinema. Gaby Schreiber wanted different moods to suit different occasions by varying the colour of the lighting. She also designed several of the delux suites.

Some of these original rooms have long since disappeared, their spaces being used for other functions. Amongst those lost were two night clubs.

The first, the Q4 Room, was designed by David Hicks, the son-in-law of Earl Mountbatten of Burma. The walls were of grey flannel and as a night club the tables had black cloths laid on them in the evening. In the day time, however, the room could be put to other uses and the table cloths were changed to ones of red and pink, providing a brighter mood.

The other night club, the 736 Room, was the creation of Stefan Buzas who also designed the London Gallery. The 736 Room could also be changed from its night time purpose and become a bar and discotheque during the day.

Theo Crosby's Observation Bar (also known as the Look Out), with its forward views of the sea, was panelled in cedar veneer. This was the only public room with such a view and has now sadly been put to another use and denied to passengers.

Amongst many other works of art on board three tapestries that faced the entrance of the Columbia Restaurant were note-worthy. These depicted the building and launch of the *QE2* and were designed by the Canadian, Helen Banynina.

Statues, model ships, paintings and many other works of art would decorate the ship. The crockery and glassware, with its special *QE2* logo, was also carefully chosen and soon became targets for souvenir hunters.

Amidst all this luxury and comfort the safety of her future passengers had not been forgotten and was ensured by many lifesaving and safety features.

There were twenty ship's boats, placed ten on either side of the liner. Two class 'A' 27-foot emergency boats, painted red, were located at the fore ends of the boat deck. Four class 'B' motor launches and eight class 'B' lifeboats were all 36 feet long; the six 40-foot cruise launches could take sixty people ashore or act as lifeboats for 80 if necessary.

Sixty-two Beaufort inflatable life rafts could each take 25 persons. In all, the life saving equipment could accommodate well above the complement of the liner. 3,200 Hart-Imco life jackets were also provided.

The fireproofing of the liner also featured strongly in the technical press.

Cunard had been given a choice of either adopting the American method of using as little inflammable material as possible or the British concept of supplying adequate water sprinklers and an inert gas smothering system where electrical and other water sensitive equipment was in use. They opted to use both.

To comply with the acceptance of the American regula-tions a reduction in the use of natural woods was implemented, although the use of this most comfortable of mediums still appeared to figure strongly in the decor and furnishing of passenger areas.

This was done by using thin 1.5mm veneers of natural wood fixed onto backings of compressed, asbestos-based sheeting called 'Marinite'. Real wood furniture was also used, especially in passenger rooms.

In all 2,000,000 square feet of 'Marinite' was used on board the ship and it was often faced with wood or plastic. The Formica company produced several patterns of textured decorative laminates, all of which had been specially designed by the designers of the various rooms and these were bonded to the 'Marinite'.

The perilous effects of working with asbestos were just beginning to be recognized and the legislation that was being introduced to protect those shaping the material had to be fully complied with.

The joiners' unions had a field day and the management found themselves with a major headache.

The 'Marinite' was produced in 8 × 4 feet sheets which were delivered to a specially fitted-out part of the joiners' workshop. The cutting and drilling machines were fitted with vacuum extractors and the men issued with protective clothing. Those working the 'Marinite' were also sent for regular and frequent chest x-rays. Off-cuts and dust from the material were carefully gathered, bagged and buried in a disused quarry on the outskirts of Glasgow. This procedure was carried out once a week.

To double the shipbuilder's responsibilities towards the health and safety of its workers a similar procedure had to be carried out on board the ship where the material was often necessarily cut for final fitting.

Sometimes even after the panelling had been fitted it had to be taken down for further work to be carried out on the systems

concealed behind it. Usually, being fragile, it broke and had to be replaced. The workmen did not mind – it was continuing employment for them as it prolonged the job which, in turn, con-tributed to the delay in completing the ship.

'Marinite' was used as a fireproof ceiling too. Instead of being hidden by 'Formica' it was concealed beneath ribbed and polished aluminium or cedar planking.

As in many work places where 'attractive' items are being used a certain amount of pilferage occurred. This is called 'squir-reling' on the Clyde and the *QE2* proved vulnerable to it.

To the shipyard the amount of 'squirreling' that took place was normal but to the Cunard staff seconded to the ship it was worrying. 'They are stealing an entire ocean liner and there is very little we can do about it', police officers told Chief Officer Bob Arnott.

Brass porthole fittings found ready exchange for a pint of the local ale in the pubs of Clydebank and Glasgow; short lengths of copper piping (often cut into length even after being installed on the ship) were easily smuggled out of the yard. One local house was raided and was found to be furnished almost entirely in 'squirreled' *QE2* material!

Light bulbs, light fittings, curtains, equipment from lifeboats, almost everything was marketable.

One of the worst cases was shown to a bedroom steward who had travelled north to view his new domain. The first class

Even with two 36-foot motor launches in place on the starboard side, the *QE2* is still far from complete. Note the small radial crane temporarily fitted aft on the Upper Deck. *Scottish Record Office*

HRH Prince Charles joined the *QE2* for her short trip down the Clyde from the shipyard to the drydock. Prince Charles is seen talking to Captain Bil Warwick and Sir Basil Smallpeice.

University of Liverpool, Cunard Archives

QE2, arranged for the ship to be opened to the public of Clydebank during the evenings. A long standing tradition would thus be maintained. (Similar 'open-evenings' were also held later at Greenock.)

One of hundreds who visited the liner, Lilian Gibson, remembers that a specific route around the ship had been laid out. This was not only for the visitors to admire the spaciousness and vastness (as well as noting the occasional incompleteness) of the ship but it was also for the benefit of the shipyard who wanted to steer their guests away from the unfinished areas which were 'a shambles'.

Visitors were still coming to the ship on the eve of departure and a namesake of the shipyard, John (T.) Brown, recalls joiners and other tradesmen still working in the passenger cabins in an effort to get as much work completed as possible. It seemed to him that 'there was still a long way to go'.

By 8 o'clock on the morning of 19th November 1968 Prince Charles was on board the *QE2* as she was readied for her first and final departure from the town that had brought her into being. A special holiday had been declared for the local townsfolk.

From the cold, dark, early hours of the morning great crowds had travelled by all means of transport to line the fields

Watched by thousands who had waited patiently in the early morning chill, the *QE2* sedately leaves her birthplace shortly after 8 am on 19th November 1968.

John T. Brown

reception area, the Midships Lobby, had been fitted with a beautiful carpet. It was there one evening at the end of the day shift: the next morning a large square of it had disappeared – cut out of the centre of the round recessed area. 'We won't come here again' a dismayed Cunard manager, referring to the yard, told the bedroom steward as they walked away from the scene.

Still, in spite of these irritations the *Queen* was fitted with £3 million worth of luxury. More irritatingly her completion date was put back.

To hurry the yard along Cunard announced that His Royal Highness Prince Charles would be at Clydebank to sail with the liner on the short journey down river to Greenock. Here, at Inchgreen, the *QE2* would be dry-docked to have the remains of her launch gear removed and to have her bottom plates cleaned and painted.

For the week before departure John Rannie, now Upper Clyde Shipbuilder's Clydebank director in direct charge of the

and shores alongside the River Clyde. Between Clydebank and Greenock an air of excitement and expectancy hung in the fresh morning air as each person patiently waited to watch the regal procession of the new gleaming liner.

John T. Brown came to watch the spectacle as he had done so on other departures. But he felt that the *QE2* was something special, and he brought along his cine camera, as well as his ordinary one, to record the event.

Captain Warwick was on board his brand new charge as she progressed down the river. He allowed the youthful Prince Charles the thrill of sounding the *QE2's* siren for the first time as the liner left Clydebank.

HRH had also been given a guided tour of the ship but, like the visitors before him, had been steered away from the unfinished areas.

The *Queen* passed round the bend at Dalmuir where the *Queen Mary*, caught by the breeze 35 years earlier, slewed round

Accompanied by her tugs, the *QE2* steams down the Clyde and to the start of her trials.   *University of Liverpool, Cunard Archives*

Once at Greenock she was carefully inched into the dry-dock and would remain there for a week, having work and inspections carried out on her underwater hull. Her rudder, internally, was maintenance free. Unlike her mighty antecedents, which had doors in their rudders for maintenance access, hers was filled with plastic foam.

The *QE2* was several months behind schedule but Cunard still hoped to have her ready for the lucrative summer season of the following year and had arranged a series of 'mini-maiden' voyages in the form of short cruises to prelude her maiden voyage proper to New York.

Each day hundreds of workmen were transported to Greenock from Glasgow and Clydebank to work on the unfinished cabins at the fore end of the ship. Feeding these men was a mammoth task but a local catering firm, who specialised in providing a service for ships going on trials, managed most efficiently.

She was due to sail on a comprehensive trial to the tropics, testing amongst other things, her air conditioning. But firstly, technical trials had to be carried out in the Irish Sea.

So, on 26th November she left Greenock for these preliminary trials which would allow a normal working-up procedure of the gearing. She achieved 164 revolutions per minute.

On 29th November the beloved *Lizzie* sailed from Southampton en-route for Florida, eventual re-sale three years later and ultimate destruction in the far-off waters of Hong Kong. The *Queen Elizabeth the Second* was the successor to a glorious precedent.

The following day, the 30th, the trials of the *QE2* finished unexpectedly. Oil fuel had contaminated the steam and feed system via the oil burner supply system and the liner had to return to Greenock. She was again dry-docked for a lengthy cleaning and decontamination period.

Her main trials to the Canaries were postponed. She had been due to sail on 4th December but, because of the unwanted extra work, this was postponed.

Cleaning completed, she left for a second trial on 17th December, finishing on the 20th. Speed had been increased to 177 r.p.m. and her full potential of 110,000 s.h.p. had been developed. She was vibration free and a new sailing date for her main trials was set for the 23rd.

Everybody was happy.

and had grounded for a few seconds, completely blocking the Clyde and causing great concern, and earning herself a place in Lloyd's daily casualty list!

Bob Arnott, later to become captain of the *Queen*, was on board as her first-ever chief officer and, as such, had been 'standing by' the liner since just after her launch. He now stood aft, in charge of the mooring lines and tow ropes.

The *Queen Elizabeth 2* steamed 10 miles down the river at a speed of around 6 knots leaving a Clydebank suddenly made empty by her departure.

As she left Clydebank John T. Brown caught a bus and raced to Greenock. He was fortunate enough to arrive in time to witness the liner's arrival there.

Off the Scottish island of Arran, the *Queen* was put through her paces. Her bulbous bow enabled her to achieve a creditable 29 knots without the tell-tale white bow wave that was usual when the old *Queens* were travelling at speed.   *University of Liverpool, Cunard Archives*

Chapter Six

Trials and Triumph

By the end of 1968 prospects had begun to look brighter for Cunard as the grievous losses of previous years turned into profit. But this was only after complex and careful husbandry of financial resources and what Commodore Marr later described as 'the sale of Cunard'. By the end of the 'rescue' of Cunard only two ships were left at sea with Q4 on the stocks.

With fewer ships to operate, employees on shore as well as at sea had found themselves without a job, the unfortunate casualties of a hard-won victory. An especially bitter pill to swallow after, in many cases, years of loyal service to the company.

QE2, the symbol in steel of Cunard's retreat from the precipice of collapse, had had her main sea trials postponed until Monday 23rd December. The company then had to quickly arrange for some of its employees to act as guinea-pigs (less colourfully known as 'stiffs' to the crew!) for the trip. The first of the 'mini-maiden voyages' that had been scheduled for the new ship was to have been a Christmas charity cruise in aid of Cancer Research. As this was cancelled due to the delay in the completion of the ship a generous contribution would be later made to the charity by Cunard.

Hurriedly, Christmases were rearranged in many households as five-hundred passengers, consisting of employees and their families, headed towards Greenock.

The trials were to be sea trials in every sense of the word and the passengers had been instructed to order anything from the menus in order to test the kitchens and the ship's novel hotel department.

This was to help 'hone-up' the organisation on board as the trial was intended to be a dress rehearsal for the liner's commercial debut, a mini-maiden voyage to be taken as a cruise due to start on 10th January 1969. This in turn, would be a prelude to the maiden voyage proper leaving Southampton on the 17th for New York. A fourth 'maiden-voyage' was also scheduled for 1st February, leaving New York for the West Indies – an early test of the fabulous liner's duel-role.

Many of the crew had transferred to the new ship from the *Queen Elizabeth* and travelled north to Scotland on a freezing overnight train. These circumstances gave some of them a foreboding for the future.

On trials off the Scottish coast, the *QE2* performed superbly. She is seen here executing a turning circle.

University of Liverpool, Cunard Archives

Two fine examples of Britain's maritime engineering: one built for peace, the other for defence. *QE2* passes a 'Resolution' class nuclear powered submarine. *University of Liverpool, Cunard Archives*

Because the new *Queen* would be away from Britain for long periods of time during cruises, the crew found that they had been given neat, two-berthed cabins instead of the old dormitory style rooms that had held from twelve to twenty men. Their new dining arrangements also ensured that they would not have to eat almost where they stood as had been the case in the past. The officers also found themselves in tastefully decorated rooms.

The provisions of smaller rooms for the crew was all very pleasant but it would eventually help to destroy the sense of community (that had come from the occupancy of the old dormitories) and which had induced such fierce pride in individual ships.

The standard of food, too, was altered. Surprisingly though, the standard of choice but not of quality for the men went, if anything, down! This was at the men's own instigation, their opinions being represented by chief steward Jimmy Smith. In the old ships the stewards, for example, had to eat what the passengers were offered; but it was all very well having superb roasts, steak, fowl, etc for dinner every day but that, it was pointed out, was not how the men ate when at home. How about steak and kidney pudding, tripe and onions or Irish stew? Home cooking was what was wanted. The company concurred.

Novel design was the hallmark of the *QE2* and this extended to the hotel staff's uniforms. Stewards were given beige jackets ('like a bush jacket!') and white polo neck jumpers. Some expected to find 'The Thoughts of Chairman Mao' tucked away

in the breast pocket! The new uniforms looked smart and were fine if the wearer was slim, but worn on torsos that were sometimes over fond of food or perhaps a few pints of good English Ale the new design 'looked . . . awful', as one bedroom steward put it. The uniforms would be changed within a year.

The new hotel organisation on board the *QE2* caused other problems for the crew. In the past passengers were served with tea and biscuits in their cabin before going for breakfast in the main restaurants; but now they could order breakfast in their rooms. This meant a double trip to a cabin: one to pick up a checked off breakfast menu and another to deliver the meal. Twice the walking!

Most of the 'teething problems' caused by the new concepts were soon sorted out at staff level but a more serious problem would soon be facing the ship herself.

For the shake-down cruise to the Canaries the shipyard had embarked two-hundred men. Mainly consisting of joiners, plumbers and electricians as well as shipyard and engineering workshop staff, it was hoped that they could complete the unfinished work in the cabins at the fore end of the ship. Upper Clyde Shipbuilder's (Clydebank) director in charge of the *QE2*, John Rannie, embarked with his wife.

Far from luxuriating in their surroundings the passengers had to earn their keep. There was still a lot of cleaning and washing down of walls to be done and the embarked Cunard staff set-to to do what they could to get the liner ship-shape.

All was going well until ten o'clock on Tuesday 24th December – Christmas Eve.

Down in the Turbine Room a small-bore pipe on a pressure gauge sited over the starboard h.p. turbine fractured, spilling oil over the ahead and astern turbine, and over the differential expansion indicator which then gave a warning, apparently due to flooding with oil.

At the same time vibration was noticed to be coming from the turbine and it was at first thought that this was due to the cold oil that was being spilt onto a hot part of the machinery.

Speed was reduced on the starboard engine as an attempt was made to account for the continuing vibration.

By 3.35 in the afternoon the vibration increased severely and the turbine was stopped. The port engine was slowed to 60 r.p.m.

The starboard h.p. turbine was inspected and this examination continued until 8.30 on Christmas morning. Two hours later the starboard engine was re-started until both engines were achieving 150 r.p.m.

This speed was maintained until 4.15 on Boxing Day morning when the errant turbine once again started to vibrate. Reduce speed was ordered once more until, twenty-four hours later, the turbine was stopped altogether and allowed to cool. Just before breakfast the turbine was again started; the vibration was still there but it was not so strong as it had been.

The problems were far from over as it was now the turn of the port side machinery to malfunction. By the early evening the vibration had increased. At 8.30 on the morning of the 28th the bridge ordered speed to be reduced as the ship was approaching her anchorage off the Canary Isles where she stopped with engines on 'Stand by'.

Just after 5 o'clock that afternoon, the *QE2* weighed anchors to proceed to Las Palmas but, as she got underway, a bumping noise was heard coming from the starboard turbine followed by a grinding crunch. After this the turbine ran vibration free, the ship reaching Las Palmas three hours later where she anchored at 8.25pm.

Immediately on anchoring Sir Basil Smallpeice and Anthony Hepper came on board having previously flown out from the UK. A meeting that would last for eight hours was then held in the Card Room with Tom Kameen, Cunard's technical director, reporting that John Brown Engineering did not yet know what had caused the damage let alone how to cure it.

Angus Gibson, one of the John Brown tradesmen on board, wrote home from Las Palmas: 'There has been trouble with the engines for the past two days. I don't think we will be getting ashore. We are only stopping for a couple of hours. The weather is quite good but not a lot of sunshine. We are working most of the time so there is not much time for relaxing. There is not much to do anyway except go to the pictures. If all goes well we should be docking at Southampton on Wednesday 1st January . . .'

The letter posted on board the *QE2* bore an ironic 'Acceptance Trials' cancellation mark.

Sir Basil Smallpeice kept the ship's company informed of events over the tannoy. Members of the press had also embarked at Las Palmas and they now sent, fortunately, mostly sympathetic and often enthusiastic reports home.

That evening John Rannie spoke to his men at dinner and asked them if they would be willing to work for another seven days at Southampton after their arrival there.

On the following day, Saturday, 'J.R.' sent a radio message to his shipyard manager, Boyd Haining, telling him that a turbine had broken down and that the ship was at anchor. The fault was major and could not be rectified at sea. To bring the ship back to the Clyde was just not practical: Southampton was the nearest suitable port.

Boyd Haining was also instructed to contact Geoffrey Moss, managing director of Cammel Laird's at Birkenhead, with a view to leasing their submarine/trials accommodation ship the *Cammel Laird*.

The shipyard manager was invited to inspect the vessel and his heart sank when he subsequently saw the result of many months of neglect. However, Geoffrey Moss recalled some men from their Christmas holidays and the vessel, the ex-Irish Sea ferry *Royal Ulsterman*, was made habitable. The *Cammel Laird* tied up at the Ocean Terminal at Southampton a day and a half

before the great Cunarder arrived at her new home for the first time (which was also her port of registration). (All the other great Cunarder's had been registered at Liverpool although they had used Southampton for many years.)

It took *QE2* three days to limp home, arriving in Southampton on January 2nd, one day later than had been anticipated. Sadly, the day before, a ship's hotel officer, George Boyle, had collapsed and died.

The planned reception for the ship that had been organised by Cunard was cancelled as the company said that it would not be 'the splendid arrival it should have been'. A launch to carry officials; hundreds of inflated balloons; the Hampshire Police Band; all were cancelled.

However, the Sotonians felt differently and they warmly welcomed 'their' new ship that would replace the former *Queens* in their hearts. The Mayor and other city officials welcomed the ship on behalf of the city and a feeling of celebration pervaded the ship and town.

John Rannie slipped quietly ashore, returning to Clydebank to complete the paperwork for the ship's completion and handing over. He was not to board the liner again for many years.

As Boyd Haining reached the top of the gang-way he was greeted by Bert Farrimond, personnel director of UCS, with the words: 'Now I know how Mafeking felt'! Boyd Haining's first job – he was responsible for personnel matters for the Clydebank division as well as being shipyard manager – was to pacify the Scottish workforce and to get their problems sorted out.

The 'Bankies' were eager to get home and many were still suffering from 'having celebrated rather too well over the festive season' (Hogmanay having occurred a few hours previously). The secretaries on board could not cope with the clamour for travel warrants or for money, hence the greeting given to the personnel manager on his arrival.

Over the next few days the situation was eased, as the workmen went home on leave and fresh men arrived from Scotland. On their arrival they found that accommodation had been arranged for them around the city; the *Cammel Laird* had

Captain 'Bil' Warwick surveys the river ahead of his liner as he takes her to sea for the first time.   *Architectural Press*

met with initial disapproval as being too cramped, especially after the men now on leave had experienced the luxury of the *QE2* whilst on trials. Berthing on the smaller vessel was later reduced by half.

More men were also flown down from UCS (Clydebank) as the turbine breakdown had provided an ideal opportunity to at last finish the uncompleted cabins. The engineering difficulties thus proved to be 'an enormous blessing in disguise' for the ship-building department as all publicity now fell on the turbine troubles and attention was diverted from the unfinished state of the accommodation.

Vosper Thornycroft sent in local squads of platers, welders and caulkers to assist with the work and daily meetings were held between shop stewards of both shipyards presided over by the shipyard manager of UCS. Fourteen-hundred men were soon to be working on the liner.

Daily meetings were also held between Cunard (headed by Sir Basil Smallpeice) and Upper Clyde Shipbuilders, represented by Tony Hepper and John Brown's technical director, John Stark.

Cunard had refused to accept the ship of course and at one time even considered selling her. Sir Basil even put forward ideas that, whilst laid-up, the ship should be hired out for private functions to help make her pay.

Relations between the two companies became increasingly strained; at one point they became so strained that Cunard decided to withdraw the facility of providing lunch time coffee and sandwiches for all staff. The shipping company had just cause to be angry. All sailings (six altogether, losing £2 million) had had to be cancelled starting with the maiden voyage, and an expensive advertising and marketing campaign written off. The crew, so painstakingly trained, had to be retained throughout the repair period and many were sent home on full pay.

By this time many heated debates had taken place in the House of Commons. David Price, Member of Parliament for the Southampton district of Eastleigh, made a plea on January 24th: 'At this moment the clear priority is for the *QE2* to be completed successfully and speedily and nothing should be said or done that would divert those concerned from fulfilling that purpose'.

During the early part of January the immediate priority of repairing the damaged turbines had been put in hand. On the *QE2's* arrival in Southampton the covers had been removed and the turbines visually inspected.

The immediately visual evidence of damage to the starboard turbine was that hundreds of blades had been stripped from the main body of the rotor hub. A complete circle of blades at No. 9 stage and several from stage 10 had been carried away and lay at the base of the casing. On further inspection cracking could be seen at the bases, or roots, of other blades. In the starboard turbine the damage was less extensive, seven blades had gone from stage 9 and there was some cracking in stages 8 and 10.

The rotors were taken out, boxed and flown back to John Brown Engineering Ltd. on 6th January, leaving the turbine room looking like 'a flour mill' after the insulated cladding had been stripped off.

A thorough investigation to assess the causes of the damage and to make recommendations that would obviate their re-occurrence was set in motion. The investigating team worked under the leadership of Sir Arnold Lindley, President of the Institute of Mechanical Engineers, and their findings were published in an important paper (by Messrs. Coats and Fleeting) that was read to the Institute of Marine Engineers.

It was found that the blade roots, which were square, did not expand as much as could be expected and that the steam supply nozzles, used to deliver steam on to the blades, were of below standard quality. There were also too many of these nozzles.

The badly damaged starboard high-pressure turbine rotor. The extent of the damage to the 9th and 10th stages of blades can be clearly seen.
Shipbuilding and Shipping Record

The resultant vibration and resonances that were induced in the blades proved to be too much and as one cracked and sheared it took away its immediate neighbour until masses of blades had been torn from the rotor.

The remedy was to provide new blades with strengthened roots and to 'tie' them together with a continuous length of one eighth of an inch stainless steel wire welded between all blades of each stage, thus providing a stiffness and a resistance to resonance.

Sir Basil Smallpeice thought that such a basic fault that had caused the damage should have been found during test-bed trials and blamed John Brown Engineering. Pametrada, the turbine's designers, had gone out of business under the Geddes committee recommendations that had streamlined so much of Britain's shipbuilding and marine engineering industry.

The port turbine rotor arrived back at Southampton by road and arrived at Vospers for inspection on the evening of Saturday 1st March.

With the arrival of the starboard rotor imminent, Sir Basil Smallpeice announced that the maiden voyage of the *QE2* was scheduled for 2nd May with proving trials first taking place, and there was no foreseeable reason why Cunard should not take delivery by the second half of April. He said that by then her accommodation would be 100% complete and there would be no doubt about the reliability of her engines: 'QE2 will more than fulfill the promises made to her prospective passengers as to her performance.' He added: 'She will be the most superb example of the shipbuilders craft the world has yet seen.' Taking another chance to market the liner Sir Basil finished: 'QE2 is certainly a new place to visit between New York and London or Paris!'

The North Atlantic was almost finished as a highway between Europe and the USA. During January there was only one sailing from Southampton by a transatlantic liner. The German *Bremen* of North German Lloyd had the windfall of taking the passengers originally intended for the *QE2's* postponed maiden voyage of 17th January. She had also picked up the passengers who should have sailed on the now strike-bound *United States* – the holder of the out-moded Blue Ribband – the fastest liner that the world had seen.

Cunard's vision of a ship for all seasons was about to be vindicated.

A typical study of the *QE2* in the Ocean Dock, Southampton, alongside the now demolished Ocean Terminal.   *Norman Jackman*

Photographed amidst the splendour of a Norweigean Fjord, the *QE2* serenely glides through the unruffled waters.   *Cunard*

Above and below: The first arrival of the *QE2* in Southampton was far from the splendid arrival it should have been as the ship limped in at slow speed. Fortunately the press was sympathetic.

Both, R. Bruce Grice

Chapter Seven

The Best

The refurbished turbines were reinstalled and the ship-builders assured Cunard that the liner would be completed two weeks ahead of the revised estimated schedule.

When all was ready in the engine room, QE2 was put through her basin trials. These consisted of various engine trials undertaken whilst the liner was tied up alongside the Ocean Terminal. To test the reliability of the main machinery overspeed tests were carried out which involved the disconnection of the propeller shafts from the engines and running the latter at higher speeds than could be expected in the normal operation of the ship.

The basin trials were happily successful. The next test would be to take the ship on a short series of trials in the English Channel, off the southern coast of Hampshire and Dorset.

So, after three months delay, at 7 o'clock in the evening of Monday 24th March the QE2 sailed at last leaving Southampton for the first time, under the command of Captain Warwick and with Jack Holt on board as pilot. Amongst those on board were two men with a keen interest in the outcome of the short sea-trials – Sir George Gardiner, chairman of John Brown Engineering and Sir Arnold Lindley, President of the Institute of Mechanical Engineers. They were looking forward to the tests with 'cautious optimism'.

The liner anchored for the night off the Nab light-tower in the eastern approaches to Spithead and the next day compass trials were undertaken. A speed of 18 knots was also achieved.

The 'swingiest fashion show ever staged' took place on board whilst the liner was underway and five-hundred press-men were embarked to record events.

As the passengers sat down to lunch the American superliner United States sailed by. As she did so one man was reported, perhaps apocryphally, as saying: 'There goes the world's fastest liner.' His companion came back with 'but not the best'! The latter's retort would soon be echoed by many.

Anchoring each evening off the coast the QE2 was put through full speed trials during the day. She also did a crash stop in which she came to halt in seven minutes, travelling one-and-a-half miles in doing so. Going astern she reached a speed of fourteen knots, sustaining this speed for a lengthy period.

Back in Southampton on the 27th the QE2 entered the King George V dry dock in the Western (also known as the New) Docks at 7.30 in the evening. It was the building of this very dock, the largest in the world when it was opened in 1933, that had finally persuaded Cunard to use Southampton as its British terminus for the Queen Mary when she was being built.

Unusually it would be from the flooded dry-dock that the new Queen would sail on her previously interrupted shakedown cruise to the tropics to test her air-conditioning.

During the day of 30th March seven-hundred invited passengers boarded the liner; in the early evening several members of the hotel staff walked off the ship. They were protesting about what they felt was excessive vibration in about ten cabins on Five Deck caused when the liner was travelling at her normal service speed of 28 knots.

The company promised to investigate the complaint (two months later, after further complaints, the worst affected cabins

were turned into staff offices whilst others were fitted with extra insulation) and the crew re-boarded the liner. The Queen sailed at 9.30pm.

During the first few days of April the Queen Elizabeth 2 proved her worth. Her passengers were more than happy with both their accommodation and the service. The engines – especially the turbines – performed superbly. Averaging a speed of 30 knots the liner, on occasion, reached more than 32.5 knots.

After reaching the coast of Senegal at about 15° latitude north of the Equator (where the passengers stayed cool in their air-conditioned paradise whilst the air temperature outside reached 90°F) the liner turned north to steam around the Canary Islands before heading once again for Southampton. She arrived back in the port on the 7th.

The next day Sir Basil Smallpeice held a press conference and declared himself 'highly satisfied' with the liner. Although she had lost an estimated £3 million because of her unhappy start,

The sheer grace of the liner's forward hull can be judged from this quayside photograph, taken as the ship safely reached Southampton after her disastrous trials. *University of Liverpool, Cunard Archives*

Slowly edged into her berth, the new *Queen* prepares for many weeks of battling between owner's and builders. *R. Bruce Grice*

Sir Basil stated 'she is being handed over to us in a better condition than I ever thought possible at one time'.

Sir Arnold Lindley was also happy with the remedial work that had been carried out on the turbines: 'I think we can regard the trouble with the turbines now as something in the past', but Upper Clyde Shipbuilders wanted to satisfy themselves that this was so. They announced that they were hoping to hand the ship over to Cunard on the 18th of the month but would first open up the turbine casings for a final inspection.

At a private lunch on board on the 14th April Sir Basil Smallpeice, his deputy chairman Lord Mancroft, Cunard's managing director John Whitworth and Anthony Hepper, chairman of UCS, entertained three-hundred VIPs including the top civic dignitaries of Southampton; representatives of the port, shipping and commercial interests; the lone, world circumnavigating yachtsman Sir Alec and his wife Lady Rose; and the last captains of the two great deposed *Queens* – Geoffrey Marr and John Treasure Jones.

It was announced that Her Majesty Queen Elizabeth II would visit the liner that she had launched twenty months earlier on the day before the maiden voyage proper, May 1st.

As previously stated the liner was to be handed over to the Cunard Line by her builders on Friday 18th March, but the official ceremony did not take place on board the ship: Unusually it took place in an office many miles away in London and occurred one hour later than originally announced.

At the same time, 1.15pm, in Southampton, the liner gave a three blast greeting on her whistle as the builder's flag was lowered and the scarlet flag of Cunard with its rampant golden lion clutching a globe was raised in its place.

The ship, at long last, belonged to Cunard.

A captain of *QE2* talks with a captain of industry. Bill Warwick chats with Sir Basil Smallpeice, the one man to whom Cunard would owe its survival. *University of Liverpool, Cunard Archives*

Chapter Eight

Royal Approval

The *Queen Elizabeth 2* was due to depart on her first voyage with fare-paying passengers, leaving Southampton on Tuesday 22nd April 1969. This would be in the form of a short cruise to Las Palmas in the Canary Islands, and was billed as the first 'mini maiden voyage' of the new liner.

Amongst the hundreds of activities taking place that would prepare the liner for her commercial debut was the consecration of the shipboard Jewish Synagogue, designed by Professor Mischa Black, and performed by Chief Rabbi Dr Jakobovits. Professor Black had declined the offer of utilising the old synagogue of the *Queen Mary* in the new ship as he considered the *Mary's* synagogue as being 'not in keeping with the modern trends of the Jewish faith'.

At 4.45 in the afternoon of the appointed day, the *Queen* sailed to the sounds of a military bank playing on the quayside as a mass of balloons was released. Hundreds of spectators watched as the liner was gently eased in Southampton Water by tugs gaily dressed overall with flags that stiffly fluttered in the prevailing gusty wind.

The cruise would last eight days and in its course would encompass the discovery and disembarkation (to a pilot cutter) of a stowaway, the christening of little James Clifton and the death of a fifty-one year old male passenger.

Arriving back in Southampton on Wednesday 30th April, the liner was prepared for her Royal visitors who would be inspecting the ship the next day. Her Majesty the Queen would be following the royal precedents set by her grandmother and mother when they had visited their mighty namesakes on the eves of their maiden voyages.

The Queen and the Duke of Edinburgh duly arrived the next morning at 11.50 am and stayed on board for two and a half hours, touring the ship with Captain William Warwick and Staff Captain George Smith who acted as guides.

Amongst the many fittings in which the Queen showed great interest were the navigational aids on the bridge. She also admired a figurehead of Britannia (the name of Samuel Cunard's first pioneer transatlantic paddle steamer) in the Britannia Restaurant. The figure, carved in yellow pine, had been presented by Lloyds of London. This 'wooden maiden' had lost her fingertips after a particularly lively party on board a few weeks earlier!

Lunch was taken in the Grill Room with the guests sitting at tables of four. The Queen sat with the captain, Sir Basil Smallpeice and the Vice-Lieutenant of Hampshire, Lord Malmesbury, lunching on melon ball cocktails, cold Avon salmon, mayonnaise, new potatoes and a green salad; strawberries and cream followed; a 1962 Montrachet was served. The Queen would later compliment the executive chef, Mr Townshend, on the meal and its serving.

After lunch the royal party walked through the lovely Queen's Room (this room had been flooded with oil during fitting out; an act of vandalism, it was rumoured, to delay the final departure from the Clyde). Lord Mancroft, Cunard's chief of marketing, pointed out to Her Majesty the bust of herself sculpted by Oscar Nemon. Although it was only a painted plaster cast, the Queen was interested to see it in the position that the actual casting would finally occupy.

Sir Basil Smallpeice recalled the conversation: 'You are putting it here, are you?' the Queen asked, 'How did he manage to finish it so soon?', Lord Mancroft explained that it was only a plaster copy. The Queen then described her seven sittings for the sculptor and how each time Oscar Nemon had been dissatisfied with his work. The Queen continued, quoting Nemon: 'That's no good' he says, and wrenches my head off!' whereupon the Queen twisted a clawed hand above a clenched fist to give demonstration of the sculptor's action, much to the delight of onlookers.

Before she left the ship the Queen remarked about the excellent condition of the vessel and expressed her hope for a happy maiden voyage that would be starting on the following day, and for a subsequently successful career for the liner.

The euphoria of the royal visit was replaced the next day by that of the *QE2's* departure for New York on her long delayed maiden voyage. The original maiden voyage to New York, that should have started on the 17th January, would have taken a circuitous route taking thirteen days via the Canaries and the Caribbean; a mixture of cruise and North Atlantic ferry voyage combining the two roles that had been designed into the ship.

Rain in the morning had failed to dampen the excitement that prevailed in Southampton and many vantage points both within and outside of the docks were occupied by people in their thousands.

Fourteen hundred passengers had been booked for this premier voyage; some people were only taking the short channel

The Oscar Nemon bust of Her Majesty Queen Elizabeth II which adorns a small alcove at the forward end of the lovely Queen's Room. The bust was altered in colouring from copper green to gold during a recent refit.
Philip Rentell

A very dismal 2nd May 1969 witnessed the *Queen's* maiden departure for New York. A good crowd still attended the event. *Southern Newspapers*

trip, but six hundred others were making the complete round voyage, obviously considering that the chance to attend this party-of-a-lifetime was too good to miss! The ship also carried nine hundred and six crew in all departments.

The liner had been scheduled to leave the Ocean Terminal at 12.30, but because of a delay caused by the handling of the baggage she was a quarter of an hour late in getting away.

The Hampshire Police Band had entertained the crowd of well-wishers on the quayside as well as those lining the railings of the liner's boat deck but, as she pulled away, trumpeters from the band of the Royal Corps of Transport played a specially composed fanfare 'Cunard Queen'.

Hundreds of brightly coloured balloons bespeckled the sky as Buccaneer jets of the Fleet Air Arm flew overhead. Arms waved as the thin paper streamers thrown from the high decks of the liner broke, the last tenuous link between ship and shore.

A bevy of small craft awaited the liner in the main stream, and tugs used their fire-fighting equipment to send plumes of water high into the air in joyous salute.

A little later as the *QE2* passed the jetties at the Fawley oil refinery, the tankers berthed there added their throaty greetings. The *Queen* responded with her siren.

Turning to port off Cowes on the Isle of Wight – always a vantage point from which to watch the comings and goings of the great liners – the *QE2* headed towards Le Havre, her next port of call.

The French harbour was delighted at being chosen as the European port of call for the new Cunarder. Up until now Cherbourg had had the honour of serving the previous *Queen's*

and a huge crowd had turned out to greet her as she docked on schedule.

The liner was handled through the agencies of the French Line (Compagnie General Transatlantique) as Cunard had since closed its own agency in France. It was a nice extension to the co-operation that would exist between the *France* and the *QE2*. It was also actually CGT who had given preference to Le Havre on behalf of Cunard.

During the two hours that the liner stayed in Le Havre one hundred passengers disembarked to return to the UK, the European passengers embarked and then the *Queen* was off – destination New York.

The maiden voyage was unhappily marred by the death of a sixty-one year old steward, 'Jack' Sharp, and his remains were committed to the sea as the liner came to a temporary halt in mid-Atlantic.

New York had prepared a welcome to outdo the departure from Southampton. Mayor John Lindsay had declared 7th May, as *'Queen Elizabeth the Second* Day' and, with a group of civic dignitaries, boarded the liner in the Lower Bay.

Bathed in sunshine and escorted ahead by the US Coast Guard cutter (which had brought out the mayor and his party) and a US destroyer astern, the *Queen* sedately approached the famous Manhattan skyline, the water around her continually churned white by the accompanying fleet of pleasure craft, tugs and river ferries.

Bob Arnott recalled a patriotic thrill derived from 'a gigantic sea and air display of twin triumphs in British design, advanced technology and engineering skills' when a 'jump-jet

Greeted by an enthusiastic crowd, (which would become typical all over the world as the Queen took to cruising), the liner arrives at Southampton assisted by tugs.   *Architectural Press*

(Harrier) hovered at each extremity of the bridge as we entered the harbour'. This surge of patriotism would find a home in many British hearts in the years to come when the ship would be welcomed in many foreign ports.

The *QE2* docked at Cunard's New York terminus, Pier 92, in the North River at just after 3 pm.

The after decks of the *QE2* provided a cascading sun trap for the passengers. Each of the aluminium framed verandah windows had been individually manufactured to suit the bevel and sheer of the ship's lines. These decks would be changed to suit a variety of purposes in future years.
Cunard

The City's Mayor, John Lindsay, said that the ship would 'continue the Cunard tradition of sailing great ships into this, the greatest port in the world, for decades to come'. Thousands of people were entertained on board the new ship as she became the 'in' place in New York with socialites and politicians of many countries counted amongst the guests enjoying the British hospitality.

The New Yorkers, like the Sotonians in Britain, had been surprised at the *QE2's* appearance. Her all enclosed superstructure gave away the comforts of an air-conditioned interior, but the funnel was the strikingly different feature of the ship. Gone was the traditional Cunard funnel of carmine red with two or three narrow horizontal black bands and a broad black top; in its place was a device that was almost a sculpture. A black pipe, protruding from a white casing, surmounted a soot and smoke deflecting windscoop that was white on the outside but painted in 'Cunard red' on the inside. The terraced decks aft of the funnel cascaded to the stern providing both shelter and sun trap; the hull itself also broke from the traditional black, being painted in charcoal grey to the contemporary British Standard of BS-9-028.

The company shade of red was also echoed in the name of CUNARD painted on either side of the forward superstructure. Deck-house sides along the boat deck, and also the bridge front, had been painted in light khaki to give additional depth. In the styling of the liner's exterior, James Gardner had done his job well.

Visitors on board were also surprised at the spaciousness of the vessel. Compared to the space allotted to each passenger on the old *Queens* each passenger now had fifty per cent more deck area. Combined with her modern decor the liner presented an almost revolutionary appearance; she was a superb blend of good and practical design.

Counted amongst the twelve hundred passengers on the return leg of this, the first voyage, was one of the principle guests at the official New York reception, Lord Louis Mountbatten.

A few days after her arrival back in Southampton Lord Louis sent an autographed photograph of himself to the officers' wardroom to 'update' the one of himself that had graced a similar position in the old *Queen Elizabeth*.

With a total complement of 2,025 the *Queen's* early voyages were somewhat underbooked, but that was put down to the season. West bound traffic was particularly under-patronised in the early days for, when the *QE2* returned to Southampton, she was scheduled to carry only seven hundred on the next trip to New York.

Amongst these were two well known personalities. The Southampton newspaper, the 'Echo', reported Peter Sellers as saying, 'it's nice to have the time to take a little rest on board. You get a little tired jetting it everywhere'.

As almost an accolade to the modern image of the *QE2* Ringo Starr, the drummer of the phenomenally popular music group the 'Beatles', was also travelling: 'It's rather like a splendid hotel – better than you get at Scarborough!'

The *Queen* sailed on her second westbound voyage on Friday 16th May, at 12.30 pm.

Outward bound through Spithead she passed through the assembled, multi-national fleet of NATO which the Queen was reviewing (making it an unique occasion as reigning British monarchs had only ever reviewed British fleets) from the Royal Yacht *Britannia*.

The liner blew her loyal greeting as she drew abreast of the Royal Yacht, Captain Warwick signalled: 'Captain Warwick and the ship's company of the *Queen Elizabeth 2* with their humble duty send their best wishes and hope that Her Majesty will have an enjoyable day reviewing the NATO Fleet'.

The after verandah decks provided a sheltered meeting place - weather permitting.

Architectural Press

A group of celebrities boarded the liner for her delayed trial cruise to Dakar and the Canaries. *University of Liverpool, Cunard Archives*

Her Majesty replied: 'I am grateful for your signal. I send you and all on board my best wishes. Bon voyage. Elizabeth R.'

The Royal interest in the liner was continued on the ship's next arrival in Southampton. On Thursday 29th May His Royal Highness Prince Philip Duke of Edinburgh paid a lone visit to the ship to present awards on behalf of the Council of Industrial Design.

Many weeks earlier when it was suggested that the awards should be presented in surroundings that epitomised the spirit of the occasion the Duke himself suggested the *QE2*.

Gaby Schreiber's theatre was chosen as the venue for the presentation of the eighteen trophies. The Duke toured the liner visiting passenger and crew areas, as well as control rooms and kitchens. He backed up his selection of venue by saying that '. . . the ship represented the culmination of the work of a great many designers in a great many fields'.

Throughout the summer of 1969 the *QE2* showed her paces and proved her worth. It would, it was realised, take time to make an impression on the source of her main market, the Americans, but meanwhile the liner put Cunard back into the realms of viability.

She proved herself worthy of the faith that had been so painstakingly placed in her. In the first six months of operation between her maiden voyage and the end of her eleventh round voyage in September, she realized a profit of £1,674,000. The plug in the drain on Cunard's resources had become a foundation on which to build for the future.

Chapter Nine

Serenity, Security and Storm

To relate each and every voyage of the *QE2* and to chronicle every incident that has befallen the liner would be beyond the capabilities of this book.

However, be it sufficient to say that the *Queen*, like so many other ships before her, usually remains out of the news as long as she performs what is asked of her: the quiet and efficient performance of her scheduled voyaging.

Safe navigation and the careful maintenance of her fiercely demanding timetable has ensured that the liner has continued the Cunard Line's enviable reputation of never losing a life during peacetime operations.

Incidents are bound to happen, of course, when a ship – such as the *QE2* – annually sails so many thousands of miles. It is usually the occurrence of such incidents that brings the *QE2* into the headlines but often these events are a result of outside influences or because of accidents happening to other vessels in which the Cunarder becomes involved, through her responding to calls for assistance.

Sea lanes, like their land-based counterparts, are safe so long as their users observe specific laws and rules. Imprudent navigation on the part of other ships may, on the rare occasion, put the *QE2's* navigators to the test, especially at the 'junctions' of popular cruise ports where ships of many flags converge – sometimes too speedily!

Like most highways, those of the sea can occasionally produce a sudden drama and one ship may call on another to assist her in her distress.

The big chance of the *QE2* came on 8th January 1972.

Whilst cruising in the Caribbean the French Line's handsome *Antilles*, white hulled with the company's deep red funnel with its black top, was sailing in the vicinity of the island of Mustique, the passengers being given a closer look at the scenery.

In spite of frantic warnings from local inhabitants the ship sailed in rather too closely and struck an uncharted reef. Her oil tanks ruptured and oil spilled into the surrounding tropical seas and, worst of all, into the liner's own engine room where it ignited.

Soon the liner was ablaze and the six hundred and thirty five people on board gave the vessel up to the flames and abandoned ship. One of the ships within capable reach of the stricken *Antilles* was the *QE2*, herself on a cruise to the exotic islands of the Caribbean. Still under the command of Bil Warwick, the liner weighed anchor from her stopover point in St. Lucia and sped towards the scene of disaster.

On arriving at the location at 10.30 pm, the *Queen* found the night sky lit in a pulsating dome of dull red by the blazing French vessel. By now the *Antilles* passengers had been transferred to the island by their ships boats and it was from here that the *QE2* picked up over three hundred survivors. Initially it was thought that many had perished but these people had been picked up by other ships from another local island.

QE2 sailed at 5:30 am and later landed her rescued at Barbados. Amongst the many messages of congratulation that Captain Warwick received was one forwarded by Cunard from the President of Compagnie General Transatlantique (the French Line) and passed on to the ship by an equally grateful Sir Basil Smallpeice: 'I want to thank you for the assistance which has been afforded to us by Cunard in the accident which struck our liner *Antilles*. Please convey to the captain of the *QE2* our deep appreciation for taking onboard passengers which our crew had evacuated and put on Mustique Island.'

Fire is the most feared of all the fates that can befall a ship at sea. For centuries many fine ships – including such maritime jewels as the *Henri Grace Á Dieu* of Henry VIII, Charles I's carved and gilded *Sovereign of the Seas* and the impeccable *Normandie* – have blazed to total ruin and ways had been sought to at least control, if not obviate, the fiery nightmare that might occur.

The *QE2* had been built to be as fire-proof a ship as possible, at the time of building conforming not only to current and potential British legislation but also to American. Fire-resistant materials and superior automatic fire extinguishing and detection equipment make the *Queen* one of the safest ships to have been built. Trained fire patrols in harbour or dry-dock ensure that the unhappy fate that befell the beautiful *Normandie* does not reoccur.

Even so, the liner has not been entirely immune from fire but these have been quickly and efficiently dealt with.

A particular engine room blaze in 1976 left the *Queen* without the use of one boiler and she limped back into Southampton with the lower white casing of her statuesque funnel blackened. The effected boiler had to be replaced by dry-docking the liner by cutting an access hole in her side to remove the damaged machinery and install its replacement. Similar damage to an

The external evidence of the blaze in which one crew member was injured in 1976.
Southern Newspapers

older ship would, perhaps, have resulted in its premature scrapping.

Fire when unchecked, can destroy even the best of Man's creations whether afloat or on land but the main cause of wanton and deliberate destruction is often Man himself.

One occasion arose during the eventful early years of the *QE2's* career and was one which would seriously affect the liner's future security arrangements – including her public accessability.

It all began in New York, May 1972. Of many evening classes being held at various locations in that bustlingly cosmopolitan city was one particular English class at Hunter College in Manhattan. A pupil of the class, Miss Barbara Shelvey, had written a short story based on a shipboard bomb scare of a previous year and Miss Shelvey's own uneventful voyage on the *QE2*.

The action of her story took place on board the Cunarder and involved two main characters who had booked passage. One character was a Mrs. Garth, terminally ill with cancer, and the other an ex-convict who found no joy in life. Their plan was to hijack the liner by holding-up the captain on the bridge at gun point and then commit a jewel robbery prior to escaping in one of the ship's launches.

Because of Miss Shalvey's shyness the evening class teacher, Professor Philip Freund, read the short story to the rest of the class. Only five students were present in the class that evening and one remarked on Miss Shalvey's 'fantastic imagination'.

A few hours after the reading a telephone call was received at Cunard's New York office, taken by Charles Dixon, Vice President finance and operations of the company's American organisation.

The caller said that unless a ransom of $350,000 was paid in ten and twenty dollar bills two accomplices, one terminally ill with cancer, and at that moment on board the *QE2*, would detonate six explosive devices, depth charges, concealed within the ship.

The FBI was called and Cunard alerted the Ministry of Defence and Scotland Yard in London. Money was obtained with which to pay the ransom in New York whilst, in England, the RAF readied two aircraft; a Hercules which would fly out a bomb disposal team and a second aircraft, a Nimrod, which would be used for communications.

The military bomb-disposal team consisted of four men – Captain Robert Williams, Sergeant Clifford Oliver, Lieutenant Richard Clifford and Corporal Thomas Jones. Together the men represented the Special Air Service (SAS) and the Special Boat Service (SBS) of the Royal Marines.

The liner had been en-route for Cherbourg (the *QE2* had reverted to using this traditional Cunard port instead of Le Havre in early May) and Southampton, but had hove-to in mid-Atlantic to embark the military parachutists. On board for Voyage 84 were 1,438 passengers including the conductor, Leopold Stokowski, and Mr George Kelly, Uncle of Princess Grace of Monaco. It was May 18th.

Captain William Law had previously arranged a search of the ship and informed the passengers of what was happening. Generally they remained calm, but one or two women, who could not apparently stand the suspense, were visibly upset.

Excited passengers lined the ship's rails to watch as the four parachutists appeared, dropping from beneath the low cloud base into the sea at the liner's starboard bow. A ship's launch under the new command of Junior First Officer Robin Woodall (later to be a captain of Cunard's Caribbean cruise-ships and later relief Captain of the *QE2*) picked up the men and brought them to the ship. After the first officer had introduced their leader, Captain Williams, to Captain Law on the bridge the army com- mander reached inside his wetsuit and produced a copy of that day's newspaper which he presented to an astonished skipper.

The military men then conducted a search of strategic points in the passenger accommodation, baggage storage rooms etc.

About an hour after the disposal team had boarded the rumours started: 'They have found two bombs already in Two Deck baggage area!', a stewardess excitedly told crew-member Barney Gallagher and his work-mate.

The bomb scare proved, as was suspected, to be without foundation and nothing was found.

The Manhattan evening class professor had, by now, heard the news of the bomb scare and realized the close similarity between his pupil's story and fact. He telephoned the police and the next day a New York show salesman, Joseph Lindisi, was arrested. He was later sentenced to twenty years imprisonment pending a psychiatric examination.

Although the whole affair had been a hoax Cunard had gained valuable first hand experience in anti-terrorist security, and ship-board security was subsequently tightened. No longer would the casual visitor be able to stroll around the ship whilst in port – and out went the traditional 'Bon Voyage' parties held by passengers in their cabins for those friends being left behind.

But as one very relieved American passenger said after the dramatic mid-Atlantic meeting between ship and security forces: 'It was very comforting to think that Britain can still reach out.'

Although deliberately induced harm has been guarded against (more than it had been in the air) the ship is, as are most types of transport, still prone to the whims of nature.

'WNA' is a marking on a vessel's load-line which indicates a special condition: Winter North Atlantic. The designers of the *QE2* did away with winter on the North Atlantic for their ship as it was planned that the ship should go cruising during this inhospitable Atlantic season. Although the *QE2* can still encounter storms on this ocean information given by modern navigational aids and computers can enable the bad weather –

May 1972 saw British military parachutists jumping into the sea near a stopped *QE2*. A bomb hoax had started a full-scale exercise which still has its echoes in the continuing security arrangements today. *Cunard*

and sometimes, in early Spring, ice – to be avoided by sailing around the affected area.

But when inclement weather is unavoidable then the force of the sea, which man can only ignore at his peril, can often leave its mark.

In April 1972, the month before the bomb hoax, one particularly severe storm lasted for several days and the *Queen* arrived in Southampton 36 hours late.

The six hundred passengers were presented with bouquets upon disembarking, leaving behind them pianos, crockery and glassware smashed by the effects of the turbulent ocean.

Captain Mortimer Hehir also presented a signed 'Storm Certificate' to everyone on board:

This is to record that on her North Atlantic voyage leaving New York on the 16 April 1972, for Southampton, England, *RMS Queen Elizabeth 2*, of 65,863 gross tons encountered exceptionally severe weather in position Latitude 42° 18' North, Longitude 55° 52' West.

During this storm, winds reached speeds in excess of 100 mph. Combined with heavy swell, waves were encountered of 50 feet in height.

This weather caused even the *Queen Elizabeth 2*, with her exceptional size and sea-keeping qualities, to lie hove to for 21½ hours between 17th and 19th April 1972, until the storm abated.

I commend all passengers in sharing this unique experience with great cheerfulness and calm.'

Mortimer Hehir
Captain

The 'uniqueness' of this particular storm was spoilt in September 1978, when Captain Douglas Ridley encountered similar severe weather which damaged the liner's fore peak railings.

The ship's size and ability to weather most seas was proven when the liner went to the rescue of a yacht, crippled in a Mediterranean storm during the season of the Mistral.

A northerly gale was blowing on 25th September 1974 when, as the *QE2* cut her way through the heavy swell of the Mediterranean between Naples and Barcelona, distress rockets were seen at 3 am. Responding promptly to the call for help and in order to avoid causing further damage to the French yacht *Stephanie*, which was in immediate danger of sinking, Captain Peter Jackson stopped his liner some way off and allowed her to drift over to the stricken vessel, thus giving her a lee in which the six survivors could be rescued from almost certain death. The flare that the captain had seen had been their last but one.

The liner then gave warning of the wreckage to other ships in the area and the next day the US cruiser *Little Rock* of the US 6th Fleet confirmed that they had sunk the remains of the yacht.

Peter Jackson was later received by the Chairman of Lloyds of London in recognition of his masterly navigation and humanity. From other authorities came silence, a strange reward indeed for such a notable action.

Danger lurks not only on the surface of the sea but also under it, waiting for the unaware navigator.

The *QE2* had gone to the rescue when an unchartered reef had caused the total constructive loss of the *Antilles* and it would be, ironically, an incorrectly chartered reef that would cause enough damage to the *QE2* to warrant her dry docking for repairs.

This happened during a Caribbean cruise when the liner was manoeuvring in the 'swinging' ground at Nassau prior to sailing. As the liner's bow turned, her underwater bulbous bow collided with a coral reef, was holed and the liner had to proceed to New York, the remainder of the cruise being cancelled.

Captain Hehir was held responsible but on the 28th January 1976, the liner's next call at the port, Staff Captain Peter Jackson, along with first Officers Sturge and Warwick and members of the ship's sub-aqua diving club took a boat and set off to investigate the reef.

To the exoneration of their captain they found, by the use of sextant readings and landmarks, that the reef had been incorrectly charted: instead of running practically straight it had two 50 foot 'headlands' and on one of these, which projected from the charted line, was found evidence of the *QE2's* collision. A marker buoy was also found to be incorrectly moored (being 130 feet away from its recorded position) and the two errors combined confounded the ship's navigators' assumption that the safe water that they had reason to expect was not there.

It is usually the *Queen's* involvement in dramatic events that ensure her of a headline and general public interest, but to the thousands who travel on the *QE2* it is the trouble-free ferry voyages across the Atlantic or her cruising to places of interest that evoke the happy memory of ports visited and sights seen.

Her winter cruising days started with forays to the Caribbean from New York but, by 1975, these had developed into full World Cruising. The *QE2* has now completed either one of these cruises or else a comprehensive Pacific cruise each year and many new and exotic ports have been added to her itinerary for the delight of her passengers.

She broke new ground for Western liners by cruising to China in 1975. On her popular visits to Hong Kong the *Queen* often takes advantage of an economic cosmetic treatment when local painters swarm over bamboo scaffolding, erected precariously on small boats bobbing around the ship, giving her hull a smart new coat of paint.

The liner's transition of the Panama Canal is always popular, with passengers crowding the rails to witness the event. The largest ship to pass through the canal, the *QE2* also pays the highest fees but the savings in fuel costs by doing so far outweighs the longer passage south. However, the *QE2* is due to round the Horn in a special South American cruise in 1989 following in the wake of the *Queen Mary* when she passed Cape Horn en route to her final destination at Long Beach in 1967.

QUEEN ELIZABETH 2

STORM CERTIFICATE

This is to record that on her North Atlantic voyage, leaving New York on the 16th April 1972, for Southampton, England, RMS QUEEN ELIZABETH 2, of 65,863 gross tons, encountered exceptionally severe weather in position Latitude 42°18' North, Longitude 55°52' West.

During this storm, winds reached speeds in excess of 100mph. Combined with a heavy swell, waves were encountered of 50 feet in height.

This weather caused even the QUEEN ELIZABETH 2, with her exceptional size and sea-keeping qualities, to lie hove to for 21½ hours between 17th and 19th April 1972, until the storm abated.

I commend all passengers in sharing this unique experience with great cheerfulness and calm.

Mortimer Hehir.
Captain

An early spring crossing of the *QE2* in April 1972 met a late severe gale. The captain had this special certificate issued to commemorate the event. Passengers were also given bouquets as they disembarked.

T.S. Gough

Attended by 'mules' on the rail tracks to either side of the lock, the *QE2's* 105-foot beam (still in her post Falklands livery) is eased through the lock-gates whilst transiting the Panama Canal. (Her maiden passage through the canal was in 1979). An expensive journey of a few hours cuts out an even more expensive alternative voyage of rounding the Horn. *Captain Borland courtesy of Southampton City Museums*

From Southampton the liner cruises to the Atlantic Isles, the Iberian Peninsula and to the Mediterranean. North Cape cruises, too, are extremely popular with the liner dwarfed by the magnificently spectacular scenery of the Norwegian Fjords as she steams in sheltered deep water between sheer mountain cliffs, cascading with pine forests and waterfalls.

During the course of the *QE2's* World Cruises her passengers have many options open to them. One of these is to join the ship for only part of the voyage and the experiences gained from such a journey can be most enriching. Owing to the cessation of the majority of the old-style, regular liner voyages a part of the *Queen's* cruise can be used as a substitute, making a visit to friends or relations that much more rewarding. Passengers can join *QE2* anywhere in the world by plane and in recent years the ship has enjoyed a unique distinction in being paired with that superb product of Anglo French co-operation, Concorde.

The list of islands visited in the Pacific – Tonga, Tahiti, Fiji, the Society Islands where one can see fish swimming in the coral from glass-bottomed boats – seems endless. Dancing to Joe Loss and other bands, discos, midnight buffets, patriotic departures from New Zealand and the gala firework welcomes in Australia (which make the British amongst the passengers proud to be British) all make world cruising in the *QE2* so popular with many people often repeating their bookings. Wry British humour on board, whilst appreciated by compatriots – 'Watch out for the bump!' as the liner crosses the Equator – can leave other passengers worried!

During one Pacific cruise of the *Queen* in the early 1980s, Alan Whicker, the television presenter of 'Whickers World', based one of his series around the liner. This proved to be very unpopular with the crew as it encroached on their private relaxation and gave, perhaps, a one-sided view of life on board – and on shore. Many people, including passengers, refused to take part in the glossy documentary.

The *Queen Elizabeth 2* is an extremely popular visitor to Japan, her arrivals there drawing crowds to the quayside numbered in thousands. Yokohama, especially, gives the liner a rapturous welcome, so much so that the city has chartered – at a reported fee of £14 million, the ship for 'Yokohama Exotic Showcase '89' which will commemorate the 130th Anniversary of the Port and the centenary of the municipality of the city. The charter will extend from March until September 1989 and will last for seventy-two days.

One particular charter was surrounded by a extraordinarily high-level of security that was, fortunately, never brought into action.

The *Queen Elizabeth 2* sailed not only into New York, in early April 1973, from a Caribbean Cruise but into the start of an intense security exercise.

The liner had been chartered by Assured Travel of Worcester, Massachusetts, run by Mr Oscar Rudnik. He had conceived the idea of chartering the *QE2* to take travellers to Israel to join in the celebrations of the Twenty Fifth Anniversary of that State's founding.

Cunard had anticipated carrying twelve hundred passengers each way but that would turn out to be the final total number for the entire voyage. Mr Rudnik had hoped to recoup his subsequent losses by using the liner as an hotel whilst she was in Israel,

Above: The *QE2* at anchor in one of the many exotic harbours that she visits during the course of her annual cruising itinary. An anchor was lost during a westbound Atlantic crossing and, in doing so, punched a six-inch hole in the Fore Peak Tank. Speed was reduced to 24 knots and the ship was diverted to Boston, Mass, where the ship was ballasted to bring the damaged area above water. A plate was welded over the hole until more permanent repairs could be made during a later dry-docking. The anchor was never replaced.

Cunard

Left: Leaving New York in the early 1980s, this photograph shows the build-up of penthouses on the Signal Deck just behind the Bridge.

Cunard

but permission to do so was refused by the Israeli government.

However, the QE2 sailed into an even tighter security net when she arrived in Southampton on April 11th. Her dock was sealed off, passes were required and scrutinised and frogmen patrolled the water around the stationary liner. Lorries were searched as they delivered stores.

Captain William Law went on sick leave with a strained back and his relief captain, Mortimer Hehir, took over. The crew each demanded £50 danger money for the voyage plus four years wages should they fall victim to Arab terrorists during the voyage.

Questions were asked in Parliament ('Who was paying for the Civil and Military security?' 'Cunard.') and the passengers (mostly American Jews who had saved for this 'trip of a lifetime') arrived in Southampton in coaches accompanied by police escorts. Fifteen men with Israeli passports reportedly boarded the ship at Southampton as did members of the SAS who would keep a low profile during the voyage guarding strategic points, such as the bridge, and keeping their conversation to the minimum with the crew with whom they came into contact. Ten members of the crew having Irish connections were put ashore in fear that they might identify the SAS men to unfriendly Irish agents. Cunard's own security people reportedly placed dummy bomb-like objects at various points around the ship which, using a percussion cap, made a loud bang if moved. The astute crew found and reported each device and, as instructed, not one of the devices was touched.

Crowds once again lined the shores of Southampton Water as the QE2 sailed on Sunday 15th April.

Her next port of call was Lisbon in Portugal. The security conscious Portuguese closed the Salazar Bridge whilst the Queen passed beneath it and the security surrounding Rochas Quay reflected the Portuguese watch against hi-jacking, ever intense since their own liner, the Santa Maria, was taken over by an anti-governmental faction several years before.

Sailing on, the QE2 passed through the Straits of Gibraltar. Here, the fabrications that emmanated from the media during this 'non event' of a danger cruise were in evidence. A radio reporter, broadcasting 'live', described naval craft coming out from 'Gib' and steaming in line ahead and astern of the liner in glorious sunshine. The ship's radio officer, listening to this report, went on deck. The 'glorious sunshine' was murk and nothing could be seen of the navy! Unhappily, this standard of reporting existed throughout the cruise and dismayed many of the crew.

The liner passed north of Malta and Crete thus avoiding the North African coast. This was done, the captain was reported as saying, to avoid the unintended provocation of the anti-Israeli North African Arab nations who might think that 'we are thumbing our noses at them'.

The liner sailed through most of the Mediterranean to Ashod in blackout. Her arrival at that port angered many Orthodox Jews as it occurred on a Saturday.

David Ben Gurion visited the ship before she left for Haifa, where she stayed for a few days, later returning to the new deep water berth at Ashod. Strict security surrounded the ship at all times with passes being thoroughly scrutinised both at the dock gate and at the ship; troops continuously patrolled the dockside and fast patrol craft were in evidence out in the open sea. Anti-personnel devices were detonated in the harbour at night around the floodlit ship in order to deter unfriendly divers.

The Queen spent just over two weeks in Israel before returning to Southampton, where the security exercise was repeated, on Sunday 13th May.

The whole charter may have passed into the realms of 'just another cruise' but for a startling revelation made one year later.

The late President Sadat of Egypt was being interviewed on the BBC television current affairs programme 'Panorama'. In it he said that he was awoken in the early hours one morning by a telephone call. The caller asked for confirmation of orders issued by President Gaddafi of Libya with whom Egypt was sharing a political and military alliance under a temporary unification of the two countries.

President Sadat rescinded the orders immediately when he found out what they were. Gaddafi had ordered an Egyptian submarine to go and sink the QE2!

The QE2 once unwittingly aided the deadly aims of terrorism when, on October 20th, 1971, the liner called in at Cobh in Southern Ireland. After she had sailed, six suitcases were found unclaimed on the quayside and a burly Irishman attempted to lift them. Unable to do so because of their weight he alerted the authorities and subsequently a cache of arms intended for the IRA was discovered.

The story was continued three years later when, after a long police investigation, a gunfight took place in the unlikely setting of Southampton. It all ended with the arrest of Gabriel Megahey, a quiet Irishman, one time stevedore and Cunard crewman, — but the head of the IRA unit in the Hampshire city.

Adventure for the QE2 there has been, but the great majority of her journeys are safe and happy voyages. Apart from charters — including one from New York to inaugurate the new deep water oil terminal at Come-by-Chance in Canada when John Rannie (the managing director of the ship's builders) travelled on the liner that he had built for the first time since her disastrous trials — the ship sails on special or inaugural trips to many ports that welcome her as an honoured guest. Some of these ports are subsequently used as frequent ports of call such as Boston which the liner visited for the first time in 1971.

The vessel was the centre of attention in her American home town of New York when, watched by millions, she opened the festivities surrounding the Hundredth Birthday celebrations of the Statue of Liberty in 1987.

In May 1982, the city of Philadelphia on the Delaware river welcomed the ship for the first time. (QE2 has visited this port on many occasions since, including one arrival detoured from New York when, at the end of a special trip to celebrate the Fiftieth Anniversary of the Queen Mary's maiden voyage, she diverted there to avoid ice in the Atlantic).

The first visit was part of the celebrations surrounding the city's 300th anniversary of its founding by William Penn. During her stay in the 'City of Brotherly Love' thousands of paying guests were entertained and fed on board the liner, helping to pay for the ship's stay there; the ship's restaurants ran an almost non-stop service.

The visit was a great success and many Philadelphians took the opportunity to sail with her back to Southampton.

It was during this voyage that the curtain rose on the most dramatic episode in the QE2's history.

The requirements of Cunard and peaceful commerce would soon be laid aside in favour of the needs of the Queen's country.

By 8 o'clock that morning the Ministry of Defence was already at work. Chief Officer Ron Warwick (son of the QE2's first ever captain) and Phil Rentell accompanied a naval representative as the latter made quick decisions on how to turn the liner into an aircraft carrier. The ship's officers were horrified to hear him say 'oh yes, I think we can chop this lot off here', referring to the verandah windows aft, and also making a suggestion that the swimming pool should be filled with cement to take the weight of a forest of red-leaded, steel flight-deck supports which would bear the load of landing helicopters.

The upper aluminium superstructure, being constructed for lightness and maximum passenger use, was not sufficiently strong enough to take the weight of the proposed 'heli-pads' so the highest steel deck was chosen to take the feet of the new supports. Quarter Deck suited the bill and the heli-pads were eventually built level with the next highest deck, forward in front of the bridge-front hatch and aft level with One Deck.

Captain Jackson arrived on board at 10 am only to find his cabin already full of Cunard officials, including Executive Captain Douglas Ridley, and people from the Department of Trade, Lloyds and Royal Naval and military personnel.

That evening at 10 pm the liner was turned starboard side to the quay. It was not until 10.30 on the morning of Thursday 6th May, that an increasingly unhappy Captain Jackson heard via a 'phone call from Ralph Bahna, chairman of Cunard, that he would be actually sailing as Master of the QE2. As he was not in the Royal Naval Reserve the liner would continue to fly the Red Ensign of the Merchant Service, thus indicating that the ship was of a non-combatant status.

In turn the captain telephoned his wife to tell her the news. He now felt that he could get his teeth 'into this project with some enthusiasm'.

That day saw the start of the work to prepare the ship for her future role as the decks were stripped in the areas that would accommodate the heli-pads.

Much furniture, paintings, sculptures, ship models and fruit machines had already gone ashore along with stores, such as the caviar, that would not be required on the voyage. Military stores flowed in the opposite direction although ammunition would not be loaded until the 9th.

Meetings were held every day both on board and in London as the conversion was satisfactorily progressed. On Saturday 8th Captain Jackson took Ralph Bahna around the ship to show him the 'general devastation and new construction'. The captain considered his chairman to be 'in a state of shock for a while'!

Over the next few days the ship took on a more orderly appearance as she prepared to take on her hundreds of expected guests. Carpets which could not be taken ashore were covered in hardboard sheeting fixed together with black tape. The names of troops were later marked on the hardboard flooring outside the cabins that they were to occupy.

Workmen from Vosper Thornycroft's shipyard worked around the clock to get the ship ready. Prefabricated heli-pads that had been constructed in advance in the plate shops of the yard were now transported to the docks. Here they were lifted onto the liner and welded into place, huge table tops on many legs made of vertical 'I' bar girders.

First Officer Phil Rentell was also a lieutenant in the R.N.R. and, on the QE2's arrival in Southampton, had gone home to Sutton Coldfield to collect his uniform. He had volunteered for the Falklands trip and had been asked by Douglas Ridley, himself a senior officer in the R.N.R., to travel south acting as a liaison officer between the ship and the naval party.

A Royal Naval preparation party came on board on the eve of departure to ensure that everything was ready for the troops' embarkation the following day.

On the morning of sailing, Wednesday 12th May, Captain Jackson arrived on board early at 6.30 am only to find that troop embarkation had already started. A 'Heads of Department' meeting had been arranged for 9.15 am with Ralph Bahna and Bernard Crisp in attendance; at 10.30 am a navigation and flying operations briefing session was held on the bridge. Peter Jackson had already studied charts of the port to be visited enroute for oil and water (Freetown in Sierra Leone) and had decided that there would be a sufficient depth of water for the QE2 to go alongside the QEII quay in the container terminal there.

As the morning melted into the afternoon troops that made up 5 Infantry Brigade still continued to ascend the gangways, entering into a world of barely concealed luxury that would be their barracks for the days to come.

Each of the units that boarded had a band or piper to play them aboard. The Gurkhas created the biggest stir – their priest blessing them as they boarded – weighed down with back-packs almost as big as the fearsome soldiers that bore them. The Gurkhas would be berthed low in the ship where they would be less vulnerable to the sea-sickness to which they were prone.

By early afternoon Royal Naval Party 1980, Headquarters Land Forces Falklands Islands and 5 Infantry Brigade were all on board, eagerly seeking their cabins or improvised dormitories before going back on deck to watch the excitement of departure.

A large crowd had gathered on the quayside and bands played cheerily. Television cameras relayed the occasion in complete contrast to the secrecy that surrounded the similar trooping movements of the Queen Mary and Queen Eliabeth to and from the Clyde during the Second World War.

The world knew where the QE2 was going and what she was carrying. The world knew that Prime Minister Margaret Thatcher meant business!

It had seemed that all the top 'Brass' wanted to come to see both the ship and the troops before the departure and the quayside alongside the ship took on the appearance of a heli-port. Lord Victor Matthews, head of Trafalgar House, arrived on board at 12.30 am. The culmination to the flow of visitors came when John Nott, the British Minister of Defence, visited the ship, moving quickly amongst the troops so that he could not be asked any awkward questions.

Although the world outside was in a patriotically festive mood Captain Jackson had not yet had his share of worries for the day.

As the afternoon built up to a crescendo of fervour, the Captain received a message at 2 pm that all was not well in the engine room. One boiler had been shut down for maintenance, and now a second boiler had developed a massive leak in its supply of distilled water, 20 tons an hour, which could not be traced.

It was essential for publicity purposes that the ship should sail on time – even on the one boiler remaining in service. So, at 1545 hrs – with Captain Peter Driver on board as pilot, a force 4 to 5 wind blowing from the south east and with three tugs made fast forward and two aft – 'Stand By Engines' was rung on the ship's telegraph.

At 1603 hrs all mooring wires and ropes had been released and the liner headed up-river, there to turn in the stream before heading down towards the Isle of Wight.

Two tugs let-go by the Brambles buoy, two others let-go a little later leaving the little Albert alone at the bow to give the underpowered Queen extra manoeuvreability should she need it. She was achieving forty revolutions which gave her a speed of seven knots.

Around half past five, two 'Sea King' helicopters arrived, their pilots skilfully testing the turbulence created by the forward motion of the liner and landed on the after flight deck.

Using an improvised swimming pool made of wood and canvas on the forward heli-pad the troops celebrated the tradition of the 'Crossing of the Line' ceremony.
Imperial War Museum

The *Alberi* released her charge at 6 pm as the *QE2* headed eastwards towards the Nab light tower.

Captain Driver disembarked onto the pilot launch at 8 pm just as the liner had the Nab on her starboard beam.

The *QE2* would anchor overnight 3 miles south of the Nab and away from the gaze of shore based sightseers. During her stay there the Admiralty tug *Bustler* came out from Portsmouth with various additional stores in the early hours of the morning.

At 8 am on Thursday Peter Jackson was advised by the engine room that the ship would be ready to sail at 9 am. The source of the distilled water leak had been detected: a valve had simply been left open! During the next hour all lifeboats were tested and swung out and the engines, too, were checked. At 9.20 the anchor was hauled up and, fifteen minutes later, the *QE2* was underway.

The troops were put through their first lifeboat drill. It proved to be quite chaotic but many lessons were learnt and subsequent drills proved to be more proficient. Because of the lower deck on which they were accommodated the Gurkhas would have to ascend several decks to their lifeboat stations. So, in case an emergency should take place and the ship was darkened, these Nepalese warriors practiced finding their way blindfolded!

Because of the vast distances to be travelled the *QE2* would need to have her oil supplies replenished at sea whilst underway. To this end an oil pipeline had been fitted on Two Deck which would take the oil to the tanks.

To practice the art of Replenishment-at-Sea (RAS-sing as it was colloquially known) the liner was due to redezvous with the Royal Fleet Auxiliary vessel *Grey Rover* later that afternoon.

Before then, however, two patients had to be flown off the ship by helicopter to the nearest hospital. As the liner was due south of The Lizard this happened to be Treliske Hospital in Truro, Cornwall. One patient had a torn Achilles tendon and the other had suspected appendicitis which turned out to be meningitis. Unfortunately this patient later died.

The huge Double Down Room became the troops' mess.

Southern Newspapers

Above: QE2 in Cumberland Bay, South Georgia, with the cross-decking of troops clearly in progress. The wintery conditions are very apparent in this rare colour view.
Captain Peter Jackson

Left: Only occasionally did a helicopter use the forward heli-pad. Trying to land at the same speed of the ship and having a 65,000 ton hotel approaching at 27 knots was a daunting prospect for many a helicopter pilot.
Captain Peter Jackson

However, the ship's nurse who accompanied the men, Jane Yelland, thoroughly enjoyed her flight and took the opportunity to relieve the hospital of as many newspapers that she could find for the benefit of the men on board the troopship *QE2*.

The *QE2* met with *Grey Rover* on schedule, a line was passed and in one minute a token ton of oil pumped from the tanker to the liner. The pipe was then blown through to clear it and the ships parted. The whole operation was a success and had only taken three quarters of an hour.

On the Friday, with the ship doing 24 knots on two boilers, Captain Jackson gave written instructions to the Chief Engineer for the passage to Freetown and Ascension. This would necessitate the use of all three boilers so efforts were increased to get the third boiler 'on-line'.

In the days that followed, the troops set themselves training tasks. Stripping down and reassembling small-arms, jogging around the deck — each unit had its own allocated time, and woe betide anyone who infringed it! — attending various lectures, or practicing firing small arms over the ship's side. Black garbage bags, full of rubbish and which were normally discharged at night,

Jokingly known as 'paraffin pigeons' to the ship's crew, the helicopters practiced using the heli-pads in readiness for *QE2's* arrival in South Georgia.
Brian Atkinson

After conducting the Sunday church services, Captain Peter Jackson (right) got himself 'fully booted and spurred' in flying kit and was taken on a flight around his ship. *Courtesy of Captain Peter Jackson*

were thrown overboard and used as targets. Greater care had to be taken with live ammunition as the ship's officers complained that the railings were being shot through in several places!

The captain and officers swapped their blue uniforms for 'whites' on the 15th as the *Queen* approached warmer waters. Also, on this day, the third boiler was brought into action and so a good reserve of speed became available.

Helicopter exercises were carried on daily. After conducting the Church Service on the first Sunday at sea, Captain Jackson attired himself in full flying kit, joined a helicopter, and took the opportunity to take some photographs of his ship from the air and to investigate a Russian Intelligence Gathering Auxiliary 'posing as a trawler'. His verdict on the flight? — 'What a wonderful experience'!

During the captain's absence, his ship was technically (as well as physically!) without a master, so Peter Jackson officially handed over the command of the liner to his relief, Alex Hutcheson.

That evening the captain joined the Gurkhas for dinner. It was their eightieth birthday and he received a lethal Kukri as a gift.

Of the actual ship's crew six hundred and fifty had volunteered to go south. The stewards were told that they would not really be needed as the army units would provide their own messing arrangements. However, many stewards did go, some of them with experience from the previous war on board the old *Queens*, and served in the officers' messes.

The crew were later to be thanked by 5 Brigade's commanding officer, Brigadier Wilson, when he said that both he and his troops had the greatest respect for them. They (the crew), he said, had volunteered whereas he and the troops had had to go to the war zone. It was, after all, their job.

At 8 am on the 18th, the bridge gave the engine room one and a half hours notice of arrival at Freetown, Sierra Leone, where they would take on fuel and water.

Two pilots boarded the ship. Although their presence was compulsory and they wore masses of gold braid on their white uniforms (plus a pair of thick heeled, bright green shoes on the feet of one of them) Captain Jackson took the ship alongside the quay himself, as he was informed by the pilots that masters usually bethed their own ships in that port!

The liner took on 1,867 tonnes of oil, completing the operation three hours earlier than had been expected, and sailed at 11 pm. Meanwhile, First Officer Phil Rentell, along with many others, busied himself in 'that old tropical tradition of watching a film on deck'! The pilots were dropped off as soon as possible as the *QE2* headed for Ascension Island.

The Equator had also been crossed and the troops had rigged an improvised swimming pool for the 'Crossing the Line' ceremony which had been extended to anyone in the vicinity of the pool, a foul smelling concoction being liberally dispensed.

The 19th brought with it the Doldrums with flat calms suddenly lashed by torrential rains and fierce, sudden squalls. Orders were received that the liner should keep 50 miles away from Ascension and that helicopters would ferry stores and personnel between the island and the ship.

Thursday 20th May marked the Christian festival of Ascension Day. On this day, in 1501, Ascension Island was discovered by the Portuguese João de Nova and now, in 1982, the *QE2* appropriately arrived at her position fifty miles to the west of the island in the early afternoon. But before she arrived another ship was sighted. Captain Jackson turned the *QE2* towards it only to find it was another Russian AIG, the *Primorye*. If he had been informed of its presence the captain felt that he could have avoided the unwanted meeting. An RAF Nimrod also reported an Argentinian ship, the *Chubut*, in the vicinity.

By three o'clock *HMS Dumbarton Castle*, normally a fishery/oil rig protection vessel, was stationed off the liner's starboard side and two helicopters transferred stores from the naval ship to the giant Cunarder.

This completed, the liner steamed to and fro off the island during the night (with an improvised black-out in force) waiting for the arrival of Major General Jeremy Moore and two hundred of his General Staff, who were flying out from the UK that night, plus additional troops and stores all of which would be shipped the next day.

Strict black-out would be imposed south of Ascension and templates for different sized windows and portholes had meanwhile been made, black plastic sheeting being cut to the various shapes. These were then taped to the hundreds of windows and portholes and Phil Rentell, acting under the instructions of Captain James of Royal Navy Party 1980, checked the results of his supervision by flying around the ship at night in a helicopter. The ship, as Captain James said, had been turned from 'the brightest star on the ocean, to the darkest'.

One unfortunate side effect of the black-out arrangements was to raise the internal temperature of the liner quite considerably, the black-out creating a greenhouse effect with the plastic wrinkling from the increased temperature.

Captain Jackson went onto the bridge at 11 pm and noted '. . . a frightening sight, to see this ship belting along at 27 knots on a black night and without a light showing'.

A rendezvous had been arranged by the higher command for Cunard's *Atlantic Causeway* to transfer various stores to the *QE2* on the 22nd. Unfortunately nobody had told the *Causeway* of the intended rendezvous and the ship initially (1 am) refused to identify herself. Eventually the container vessel asked the troopship, 'for what reason do we have the pleasure of this visit?'

The two ships steamed in company, still in the vicinity of Ascension Island, and helicopter transfer of stores started at 7 am, finishing about three hours later.

The *Queen* soon left the *Atlantic Causeway* (the sister ship to the *Atlantic Conveyor* that would be sunk three days later by the Argentinians) and Ascension far behind as she increased speed on completion of her tasks and she soon left Ascension far behind.

That night black-out was rigorously enforced, navigation lights and radars were switched off, and the ship became electronically silent: the latter precaution to deny a homing signal to enemy missiles. Navigation would now rely on the 'Mark 1 eyeball'!

As the *Queen* headed south it was initially thought that she would effect a rendezvous with the *Nordic* and *Baltic* ferries between South Georgia and the Falklands.

Alex Hutcheson took the Church Service on Sunday 23rd as the captain had, like many others on board, gone down with the 'flu' and had retired early.

Exercising of all kinds still continued with special attention being given to life saving and its associated appliances.

The regimental evenings that had been held ceased as the *Queen* approached the war zone. These unit dinners had been great fun with speeches and presentations, but the regimental bands playing within the confines of the Theatre Bar or the Q4 Bar provided a sound that had to be heard to be believed!

By the 25th the *QE2* had sailed far enough south of the Equator to meet the approaching winter chill of the Southern Hemisphere. Once again the officers changed uniform, returning to wearing their warmer 'blues'.

Browning automatic guns were placed on the mounting platforms that had been constructed on each bridge wing during the voyage down and Blowpipe missiles were fitted around the funnel. The *Queen* was now in a very small way, prepared for what she might meet.

The ship was, by now heading towards a rendezvous with the battle scarred County Class destroyer *HMS Antrim* in a position ninety miles north of South Georgia.

During the night of 26-27th May the radar was switched on, briefly, every thirty minutes and at 11 pm two stationary 'targets' were seen on the screen, five miles to port. Icebergs!

Captain Jackson was called at half past two in the morning. It was flat calm and many targets were seen on the radar screen (the captain later wrote: 'No way could it be a fishing fleet!') and the ship was put on Ice Routine. At one time more than a hundred bergs could be seen in the illuminated sweep of the radar arm and the captain ordered a reduction in speed as the *QE2* weaved around the ice: '. . . don't want to be the *Titanic* of the South Atlantic' he wrote, '. . . never have I known such a harrowing experience'.

The reduction in speed meant a late meeting with *HMS Antrim* but the delay had been justified. Morning light showed thick fog, becoming patchy, and a radar check at 11 am indicated *Antrim* to be nineteen miles away.

Three quarters of an hour later the two ships had stopped within one mile of each other, and the transfer of Major General Moore, Brigadier Wilson and their staffs commenced.

On the first full day at sea *QE2* rendezvoused with RFA *Grey Rover* to rehearse 'Replenishment at Sea'. A token ton of oil was taken on board from the oiler to prove that the operation could be successfully accomplished. *Captain Peter Jackson*

Whilst sailing off Ascension the *QE2* received Major General Jeremy Moore who arrived from the island by Chinook helicopter. *Captain Peter Jackson*

Arriving at South Georgia the *QE2* began to 'cross deck' her cargo of troops by requisitioned trawlers and 'VERT-REP' stores by helicopter.

Imperial War Museum

The sea was undulating in a long swell and although the senior officers, 'cross-decked' by helicopter, other troops had to transfer by ship's boats.

The swell caused a great strain on the bed plates of the Cunarder's davits and at least one was damaged. The troops had to jump to get on to the *Antrim* and in doing so one soldier broke a leg.

The transfer operations were over by 1.40 pm and the *QE2* sailed on, still amidst patchy fog and ice. The temperature at noon had been 3°C. Hundreds of icebergs had been visible since the rising sun had bathed them in changing colours of red and gold, until their 'tablecloths' of fog had cascaded over their sides to eventually obscure them. The numbers of icebergs had decreased as *Antrim* was closed but steadily increased once again as the *QE2* left the rendezvous position. One particular berg was reported as being three hundred feet high and a mile long!

Black darkness fell at 5 pm and, just after 6 pm, South Georgia was visible on the radar. The Right Whale Rocks were discerned and half an hour later two shackles of starboard anchor cable were let out. These hung, suspended from the hawse pipe into the deep water, in readiness for the final anchoring. If all the required shackles were paid out at once the force would have torn the cable clench out of the chain locker structure and the anchor lost.

The anchor was finally let go just after seven in the evening as the liner entered Cumberland Bay. Philip Rentell was in charge of the mooring party and from his position on the prow of the ship could not see the bridge in the prevailing murk, even though lights were now on. Ten shackles of cable were let out in a shower of sparks and rust. Only two were left in the locker by the time the cable brake took its hold, bringing to a halt the heart-stopping rattle that exuded from the liner's hawse pipes.

Canberra had been waiting impatiently for the *QE2* for several hours in the confines of the bay. The rust-streaked P&O liner had seen much action in Falkland Sound and her crew were becoming veterans of the sudden air attack. The liner had on board survivors from the sunken *HMS Ardent* and would transfer these to the *QE2*. The latter ship would in turn transfer, by boat and helicopter, her cargo of troops and stores.

The requisitioned trawler *Cordella* came alongside at 9.20 pm and left for the *Canberra* with the first batch of troops just after 11 pm.

Just before midnight *HMS Leeds Castle*, the *Cordella* and the Admiralty tug *Typhoon* came alongside to take off the last troops for the night, operations ceasing until morning as the combined perils of darkness and black-out made safe navigation and working imprudent.

From one captain to another.   *Courtesy of Captain Peter Jackson*

To Captain Peter Jackson with Many Thanks from all in ENDURANCE Nick Barker.

From six o'clock on the morning of Friday 28th May baggage, stores and troops were once more transferred to the waiting ships, either by sea or by air. The sea transport consisted of the *QE2's* lifeboats, the trawlers *Cordella*, *Junella*, *Northella*, *Farnella* and *Pict* (collectively known in naval parlance – along with other requisitioned ships including the *QE2* – as STUFT, or Ships Taken Up From Trade). The air transport was by many lifts by the helicopters, their operation being called 'Vertical Replenishment', or VERT-REP.

As well as the *Canberra*, the North Sea ferry *Norland* was also waiting for troops. HMS *Endurance*, the British Ice Patrol ship, was also in Cumberland Bay, maintaining a naval presence.

Canberra sailed at 10.30 pm after taking on hundreds of soldiers and the *QE2's* Sea King helicopters, in turn transferring the survivors of HMS *Ardent* to the care available on the *QE2*. *Norland* had similarly brought men from the sunken frigate *Antelope*. Work continued throughout the night and at four in the morning snow began to fall, covering the *QE2* in a thin white sheet. This, and the presence of patchy but dense fog caused the captain to remark 'what a climate!'.

Saturday, a Cunard cargo ship, the *Saxonia*, arrived for cargo and the Royal Fleet auxiliary *Stromness* brought yet more survivors, this time from the Type 42 destroyer HMS *Coventry*. The *Stromness* would afterwards take on the ammunition for which *Canberra* did not have time to wait.

The *QE2* had not remained immune from damage during her stay in South Georgia, but fortunately this had not been suffered as a result of the conflict. The platform lifts that descended from the boat deck to the sea were damaged by trawlers coming too heavily alongside and more davit bed plates were cracked during boat retrieval operations. The day before a badly corroded pipe in Seven Deck swimming pool had burst causing a widespread flood, damaging the Sauna, darkroom, working alleyway, crew quarters and the laundry.

During the day icebergs drifted into the entrance of Cumberland Bay and then, as if realising that their presence created an anathema, drifted out again onto the wanton highway of the wintry South Atlantic.

A group of crew members were taken ashore for a look around the derelict whaling station of Grytviken. Captain Jackson

The *QE2* steamed slowly up the English Channel to ensure that her meeting with the Royal Yacht *Britannia*, carrying Her Majesty, The Queen Mother, happened on time. With survivors from *HMS Coventry* on the forward heli-pad, *HMS's Ardent* and *Antelope's* survivors aft and the *QE2's* own company on the Boat Deck the liner exchanged greetings with the Royal Yacht.
Courtesy of Captain Peter Jackson

was to have gone ashore with them but changed his mind: on his late visit to the bridge on the previous evening he had noticed that the barometer had started to fall so he was now anxious to get the last of the troops off his ship before the promised deterioration in the weather set in, an harbinger of the fast approaching winter.

By four o'clock in the afternoon a north westerly gale was making conditions hazardous: the last sixty men disembarked into the trawlers which were having problems in mooring safely without breaking their ropes. *Junella* was to be the last ship alongside, taking off stores and as soon as she left, at 5.30 pm, the *QE2* started to weigh anchor.

Passing by Banff Point fifteen minutes later the liner increased speed to 18 knots.

Two hours later *QE2* was again in the icefield but, with judicious navigation, she emerged safely at 10 pm;

Lifeboat practice was held on Sunday but the warship survivors were initially unhappy about congregating in the liner's aluminium superstructure, but their fears were allayed by the supervising officers.

Monday was a very uncomfortable day at sea and only the forward set of stabilisers was used. Two drums of hydrochloric acid broke loose in Two Deck baggage room and the chief officer was sent to get them under control.

Just under nine hundred tons of fuel oil were left in the tanks by Tuesday, enough only for a day and a half's steaming.

To replenish the ship, arrangements were made to rendezvous with the *RFA Bayleaf* and the two ships met in the late afternoon.

The sea was too rough to allow the operation to commence and as it would soon be dark the *Bayleaf* took up an overnight station astern of the *QE2*.

The RFA drifted away from the *Queen* during the night and it was not until nine the next morning that a line was transferred between ships and the refuelling commenced. When the oiling had been completed by 6.30 nearly four thousand tons of top grade admiralty oil had been given to the *QE2*. The operation (carried out in a westerly Force 7 with an accompanying rough sea – although the sky was bright but cloudy) had finished just in time as the chaffing caused by the two ships' movements had caused the connections on the *Queen* to be worn to a point of danger.

In the early evening the captain received a message to say that the *QE2* was to proceed to Southampton and at 7 pm Captain James R.N. told the crew. Many were disappointed as they had anticipated that the *Queen* would put the survivors ashore at Ascension and then return to the war zone. The news was not released in Britain until 6th June, by which time the liner had left the danger zone after stopping off at Ascension.

After their various ordeals the survivors from HM Ships *Ardent*, *Antelope* and *Coventry* relaxed in the free days at sea taking benefit, as many other people do, from the refreshing regime of a sea cruise. Gradually their spirits picked up and eventually they organised a bawdy 'Sod's Opera' which they performed in the Double Down Room to popular acclaim.

Ascension was reached on 4th June, and *HMS Dumbarton Castle* once again met the liner. The *QE2* was once more on her way by 6 pm after a three hour stay during which time the *Dumbarton Castle* had taken off personnel including six SAS men who had survived a helicopter crash on the South American mainland. A public landing in Southampton would have been against the interests of their security.

By now it was known that the Queen Mother wished to greet the *QE2* as the liner returned to the United Kingdom on Friday 11th June.

The naval survivors possessed only the clothes that they were rescued in or had been given by the liner's company. So flying stations were sounded and a helicopter flew off the ship as she steamed near Mount's Bay, Cornwall, on 10th June.

New uniforms were brought out to the ship (plus a liberal supply of fresh Cornish pasties!) and both naval and civilian personnel readied themselves for their royal reception.

Several visitors were flown out to the ship on the bright Friday morning of the *QE2's* homecoming.

At seven in the morning forty newsmen arrived on the ship followed at eight by Admiral Sir John Fieldhouse and Lord Matthews and half-an-hour later by Ralph Bahna. The pilot, Captain Driver, came aboard at 8.48 am.

A message was received from the Royal Yacht *Britannia* from which H.M. The Queen Mother would welcome the ship:

'Captain P. Jackson.

I am pleased to welcome you back as *Queen Elizabeth 2* returns to home waters, after your tour of duty in the South Atlantic. The exploits of your own ship's company and the deeds of valour of those who served in *Antelope*, *Coventry* and *Ardent*

have been acclaimed throughout the land, and I am proud to add my personal tribute.

Elizabeth Regina, Queen Mother.'

Captain Jackson replied immediately:

'Please convey to Her Majesty Queen Elizabeth, the Queen Mother, our thanks for her kind message. Cunard's *Queen Elizabeth 2* is proud to have been of service to Her Majesty's Forces.

Jackson. Master QE2.'

The *QE2* passed the famous Needles lighthouse on the western tip of the Isle of Wight at 9 am. Fifteen minutes later, after passing between Yarmouth and Hurst Castle, the Royal Yacht *Britannia* was abeam and, as the liner steamed by the Royal Yacht, the figure of the Queen Mother could be seen, dressed in pale blue, on its after deck. The *QE2's* company and the warship survivors gave three cheers and the liner blew her siren in salute.

From the *QE2* to the Royal Yacht:

'Please convey to Her Majesty Queen Elizabeth with humble duty the Master, Officers and ratings of the Royal and Merchant Navies embarked in *QE2*, join in offering their loyal greetings.'

The *QE2* was almost home. Surrounded by small craft, buzzed by light aircraft and watched by thousands lining the Solent and other vantage points she progressed in state past Calshot, then by the tankers at Fawley which, once again, blew their own greetings. She slowly sailed up Southampton Water to the Queen Elizabeth II terminal in Southampton Docks.

From the quay a sea of faces watched the liner, many looking for loved ones, and banners held high bore messages of greeting. The *QE2* was turned in mid-stream by her tugs and at mid-day came to rest, port side along the jetty.

After steaming 14,967 miles and consuming 10,287 tonnes of fuel, the *Queen* was home!

Elizabeth R

Luncheon
on the occasion of the visit of
Her Majesty Queen Elizabeth,
The Queen Mother,
on board Queen Elizabeth 2
to unveil the South Atlantic Plaque,
2nd December 1982

Host: The Lord Matthews

Luncheon

Coquille of Fresh Lobster

Roast Saddle of Southdown Lamb

*Fresh Broccoli Spears,
Parisienne Potatoes*

Fresh Pear, Liqueur Sauce

Petits Fours

*Selection of
English Cheeses with Celery*

Coffee

Wines

*Batard Montrachet 1980
(Moillard)*

*Chateau Gruaud Larose 1966
Second Growth St Julien*

Her Majesty Queen Elizabeth the Queen Mother signed Captain Jackson's menu after a very special luncheon held on board.
Courtesy of Captain Peter Jackson

Chapter Eleven

The Brightest Star on the Ocean

Following her trooping duties in the South Atlantic the *Queen Elizabeth 2* had to be refurbished, reconverting and renovating her once again to 'the brightest star on the ocean'.

Before disembarking at South Georgia the troops had cleaned the ship as best they could, removing marks where boots had scuffed the bulkheads and so on. But the helipads had to be removed at Southampton, and Cunard took the opportunity to re-style some of the rooms.

The work of converting the liner to a troopship had taken a mere eight days but this would now take nine weeks to put right. *QE2* spent much of the time in the King George V dry dock in Southampton prior to being berthed alongside a quay in the New Dock, receiving the final touches there.

She emerged from the refit ready for her first post Falklands sailing on 14th August with a pleasant alteration to her appearance. Her funnel casing that had previously been painted white now reappeared in the traditional Cunard colours of red with two, eight inch black stripes, the inner tubular casing providing the black top. Each of these bands was made up of two widths of four inch tape, soon to be flapping in the Atlantic breeze.

But the immediate impact to the eye was in the colouring of the hull. The dark, almost black, charcoal grey had been over painted with a light 'pebble' grey. Apparently so painted on the instructions of Lord Matthews, chairman of Cunard. The paint scheme proved to be unpractical as well as unpopular, soon displaying scuff marks from the nudging bows of New York tugs and unsightly streaks of rust that dribbled down the vessel's sides from portholes and anchor hawse pipes.

The liner thankfully reverted to her original hull colour of charcoal grey a few months later. To the ship-lover she then almost wore the traditional colours of the old Cunard ships and more than ever deserved, through livery and action, the title of *Queen*.

Internally, changes had been effected to maintain the *QE2's* position as leader amongst cruise ships. The Six Deck swimming pool became part of a prestigious 'Golden Door' fitness complex, expensive to use on shore but freely available to the ship's passengers. The exclusive Queen's Grill was enlarged, as was the Casino, and a start was made on the creation of a Club Lido on the aft area of Quarter Deck. This lido would be completed in Germany during an extensive refit in late 1983 when a Magrodome, a retractable glazed sun-roof devised by MaeGregor-Navire (a company familiar with special hatch covers), was fitted over the first class swimming pool making the area habitable during even the early and late Atlantic seasons.

Many bands, large and small, professional and amateur, often entertain the *QE2's* passengers from the quayside. The Highbury Area Band from Portsmouth play the *Queen* away shortly after her return from the Falklands.
Steve Dymock

It was during this particular refit that the aft verandah windows were substantially altered and new, large capacity enclosed luxury motor boats, carried on heavy davits, were fitted at the aft end of the boat deck.

The QE2's built-in ability to accept change has been proven on several occasions, the design of her internal spaces lending themselves to alterations in function or arrangement.

Amongst the many changes that have been effected over the years the early alterations were the ones that would cause most comment as, during the course of the work, some of the orignal rooms disappeared making way for new.

The London Gallery, once used as a display area for British art, eventually became the Computer Learning Centre. Once American restrictions on casinos had been lifted the spaces occupied by the Upper Deck Library and the Port Foyer found themselves amalgamated into one in 1972 to cater for the new demand. The Lookout Bar, the only public room to have had a forward looking view, was unfortunately sacrificed to become a kitchen for the new blue and white Queen's Grill, (latterly a casino but formerly the 736 Club which had been described as 'noteworthy' by the shipping press), that would cater for the occupants of the newly fitted luxury penthouses.

These penthouses were fitted in three stages and in three countries, over a period of fifteen years. The preparation for the fitting of the first of these luxury rooms took place whilst the liner was still at sea in early 1972 in readiness for when the QE2 would be taken out of service in October for her first major refit.

The prefabricated aluminium blocks of luxury cabins (which included the Queen Anne and Trafalgar suites in which the occupants had the distinction of being able to go upstairs to bed) were fitted in two halves, port and starboard. During the same refit other luxury cabins were built on Boat Deck sites previously occupied by shops and store rooms, and the old Grill Room became part of an enlarged Columbia Restaurant. The Britannia Restaurant underwent a change of name and re-appeared as Tables of the World. In 1987 the restaurant underwent another change becoming the Mauretania Restaurant.

The second smaller block of rooms, sited immediately aft of the mast, was fitted in Bayonne, New Jersey, in 1977, resulting in the Queen Mary and Queen Elizabeth Suites. The third block, aft of the first and forward of the funnel, was fitted in the most recent reconstruction in Germany in 1987.

The £2 million refit of 1972 also saw other major changes carried out, the principle work being the reconstruction of the Main Kitchen to one of a highly sophisticated American design. Minor bulkheads were erected, new tiled floors laid, stainless steel fittings and old ovens were replaced and new windows cut during the course of the work. The addition of the new windows spotlighted a serious problem in the reconstruction work. The daylight that now filled the new kitchen shone through a fine, powdery mist. Much to the horror of the workforce, this was found to emanate from the American insulating sheeting being used which, unbeknown to the men using it, was asbestos based, the necessary precautions not having been taken - until then!

Because of the difficulties in fitting out the American kitchen, the seven week refit took rather longer than had been anticipated, the liner finally leaving Southampton two and a half days late. To Cunard's annoyance Vosper Thornycroft had not given notice of the delay until ten hours before the original time of sailing. However, the ruffled relationship between the two companies was soon smoothed and Cunard admitted to being delighted with the work.

Because of all the work carried out on the passenger areas the gross tonnage of the liner has risen over the years. When the ship was still being built it was expected that she would be 58,000 gross tons but, after the restructuring of classes during building, she appeared at 65,862 tons.

The liner, after many modifications, is now 67,139 gross tons and although larger purpose built, light draught cruise ships have been, or are planned to be, constructed, she is still one of the largest true transatlantic liners ever to have been built.

The run-up to the notable changes that were effected to the Queen Elizabeth 2 in 1972 had their beginnings in the latter half of 1971 when a great change happened to Cunard itself. In spite of a poor financial year in 1970 Cunard was doing well but, due to various factors, the company found itself at the centre of a takeover bid.

The successful bidder from several contenders, buying the company for £26 million, was Trafalgar House. Already owners of civil engineering concerns, hotels and industrial activities (amongst many others) the company would add Cunard to its list of hotel interests.

Victor Matthews became the new chairman of Cunard and Sir Basil Smallpeice transferred to the board of Trafalgar House. He remained there for five months after the last board meeting of Cunard was held as an independant company, on 25th August 1971.

Sir Basil found that, after rescuing Cunard from near collapse, he could no longer effectively assist the company in his new position and 'let myself quietly over the side and went ashore. . . . . with sadness in my heart. . . .'

Since the early years QE2 has enjoyed Royal patronage and in September 1988 will be the venue of a special lunch which will be attended by H.M. The Queen Mother. This will be to mark the 50th anniversary of the launch of H.M.'s illustrious namesake, the first Queen Elizabeth, on 27th September 1938 and amongst the honoured guests, both at the lunch and subsequent commemorative voyage, will be the liner's last captain, Geoffrey Marr.

The Queen Mother was previously on board in May 1986, meeting retired Cunard employees and passengers who had sailed on the Queen Mary's maiden voyage fifty years earlier. The liner had then sailed on a voyage to commemorate the debut of that remarkable ship, Britain's best loved liner, carrying along with the veterans from that premier trip the Mary's last skipper, Captain John Treasure Jones.

After the QE2's return from the Falklands the Queen Mother expressed a wish to visit the liner that she had greeted on its return from active service. This she did in December 1982 and took the opportunity to unveil a plaque on which was engraved the message that she had sent to Captain Jackson welcoming him, the ship and the ship's company and passengers back to the United Kingdom.

Three weeks after the liner's reintroduction into service after the Falklands episode the QE2 broke down off Falmouth. It was one more in a series of engine breakdowns that were becoming both increasingly expensive and worrying to Cunard.

One of the more dramatic breakdowns had occurred in 1974 whilst the QE2 was on a south-bound cruise from New York. The causes reflected an incident that had called a halt to her technical trials from Greenock in 1968.

The liner had left New York for a cruise to Bermuda on the evening of Saturday 30th March 1974 with 1,648 passengers on board, including almost 800 senior citizens, and 1,041 crew.

As soon as she was out into the open waters of the Atlantic she ran into rough weather, rough enough to prevent the pilot from being landed. Speed had to be maintained; to decrease it would have nullified the effect of the ship's stabilisers.

Conditions were very much the same on the following day and the captain, Peter Jackson, cancelled the obligatory life-boat

With the twin towers of the World Trade Center dominating a receding Manhattan skyline the *QE2* heads for the open sea. *Cunard*

drill, the prevailing conditions making it dangerous for the passengers, especially the elderly, to try to reach the Boat Deck.

Captain Jackson also made a broadcast (his maxim was 'always keep passengers informed', and to tell them: 'If you hear rumours, ask whether the perpetrator had got it from the captain!') and advised the passengers to stay in their cabins. To this end he took the unusual step of cancelling the Sunday divine service due to be held in the Theatre.

During the evening, as the liner travelled further south, the weather moderated. It was hoped to hold the cancelled boat drill the next day.

These plans were rudely shattered when, at four o'clock the next morning (1st April), the ship came to a standstill in the water.

The captain was told that, because two pipes (one oil, one boiler feed water) had been wrongly connected, oil had contaminated the boiler feed water - water which has to be extremely pure, four parts in a million.

Fortunately by now the weather had calmed and the engineers set to in cleaning the system, working hard all day. The captain made many telephone calls to Cunard and once again cancelled the delayed boat drill considering that, under the current circumstances, it would have an unnecessarily negative psychological effect on the passengers - especially the elderly.

The liner continued to drift and the telephoned remedial action suggested by Cunard's technical department in London was effective for only half an hour.

By Tuesday morning the liner had reached a position of 29° 26'N, 68°06', approximately 275 miles south west of Bermuda.

Oil was still contaminating the port boiler and there was at least another ten hours of cleaning to do. Because of the situation much of the liner's hotel services had been shut down; the air-conditioning was shut off; the lifts were not operating (these were essential for the old folk); refrigeration had been switched off, the kitchens ceased to fully function and lighting was kept to a bare minimum. But it was the cessation of the operation of

Threading her way through the 1977 NATO Fleet Review the *QE2* provided an elegant splash of colour amongst the various shades of grey of the parading warships. *Southern Newspapers*

the desalination plant that supplied the ship's hotel services' fresh water (there was only five days supply left much of which would be used to flush through the contaminated machinery) that caused the greatest concern.

The captain knew that the nearest available large tug was 600 miles away so he put a suggestion to Cunard.

As a result of the captain's recommendations, which were approved by Cunard, the Norwegian cruise liner *Sea Venture* was sent to assist the *Queen*.

For this to happen special dispensations had to be sought from both British and Norwegian authorities. The *Sea Venture* was licensed to carry 600, only a fraction of the *QE2's* complement, but arrangements were made to cover any discrepancies both in legal and amenity aspects. In the end, the *Venture* was sanctioned to carry an extra 1,000 passengers.

The white Norwegian knight in the form of the *Sea Venture* arrived on the scene at three in the morning of 3rd April, ready to assist the distressed *Queen*.

The one way transfer between ships (almost anticipating the movements occurring during the Falklands campaign) started at 4 am with life jackets and twenty life-rafts from the *QE2* going over to the Norwegian ship to bring the *Venture's* life-saving capability up to legal requirements.

Essential stores followed and, at 7.30 am, the first passengers descended the forward and aft starboard accommodation ladders to board the waiting launches that had been lowered from both liners.

By 3.50 in the afternoon the last of the passengers had disembarked from the *QE2* and an hour later the liner had recovered her boats. The *Sea Venture's* launches continued to transfer stores and baggage until 5.40 am when she hoisted her boats from the sea, sailing for Bermuda ten minutes later.

A total of 1,654 people had been transferred during one of the most unusual operations ever carried out at sea. This number, incidentally, included six crew members who would help with the disembarkation at Bermuda.

The next day two tugs, *Elizabeth Moran* and *Joan Moran*, arrived at 2.13 pm and, seventy five minutes later, started the tow.

As the *Queen* and her entourage approached Bermuda the pilot boarded and two more tugs, *Bermudian* and *Faithful*, came to assist in the liners' passage through the Narrows to Murray's Anchorage.

Here the boilers were purged and the *QE2* was able to sail for New York at 16 knots using two boilers.

After further work at Todd's shipyard the *QE2* sailed for Southampton, still only on two boilers but achieving 24 knots. The voyage home took six days instead of the usual five.

On the liner's initial technical trials from Greenock in 1968 her engines had performed well; her pilot described her as 'handling like a motor car'.

But from the breakdown of the turbines during the ensuing full-scale trials to the Canaries to the breakdown off Falmouth, Cornwall, just after her return to service after the Falklands the engines and boilers have proved expensive to maintain. Many spare parts have had to be specially made by hand and this costly maintenance, along with the astronomic increases in oil fuel prices since the ship was built and high manning costs, caused the Cunard Line to appraise the future of the *QE2*.

They came to a momentous decision.

The *Queen*, if she was to be economically viable and if she was to continue to sail for another twenty years, would have to be re-engined.

Although extremely expensive this would be far cheaper than building a new, similar vessel.

After the initial decision was made a meeting was held in Southampton in mid 1983 to which various contenders from ship-building and engineering firms were invited. Each firm then submitted ideas and tenders for the forthcoming mammoth conversion with Cunard placing the contract with their final choice - the German shipyard of Lloyd Werft in Bremerhaven.

This yard had converted the giant ex-French transatlantic liner *France* into the Norwegian cruiseship *Norway* during the winter of 1979; the yard had also done previous work on the *QE2* including the fitting of the retractable Magrodome and the fitting of a new bulbous bow.

Cunard had for several years favoured foreign yards for the refits of their flagships. British yards had for a long time been shedding expensive manpower and were therefore able in recent years to perform only the lesser tasks in ship repair and maintenance. Unions and public bodies took this export work as a snub to Britain but Cunard had, in between, spent £millions in the U.K. in keeping the liner at sea.

British firms would, on this occasion too, be awarded many of the major sub-contracts that would emanate from the forthcoming conversion. Foremost amongst these would be firms belonging to the giant General Electric Company (GEC). It was part of this company, that under its original title of Associated Electrical Industries (AEI) that had built much of the *QE2's* original electrical machinery, such as the three turbine generators then the largest afloat.

It now fell to AEI's successor, GEC Large Machines Limited of Rugby, to build the two 350 ton, 44 megawatt electric propulsion motors, as the liner was to be converted from steam to diesel-electric propulsion. GEC Turbine Generators Limited, Stafford, would build nine electric generators and the company's Industrial Controls division, also at Rugby, would provide the synchro convertors that would start the motors and provide the slow speed operation of the ship. The engine control room console would be supplied by GEC Electrical Projects who would also co-ordinate all the company's efforts.

The turbine generators would be fitted alongside their power source, nine MAN-B&W diesels, which would be fitted five in the after engine room and four in the forward. The work of installing diesels, associated machinery, fuel treatment plant, generators and motors, would be likened to open heart surgery.

The contract to convert the *QE2* was signed on 24th October 1985 which gave Lloyd Werft almost a year in which to organise their own subcontractors - there were fifty major ones - and to advance their own preparations for the conversion.

QE2 arrived in Southampton for the last time as a steamship on October 25th before leaving for Bremerhaven. Cunard's magnificent flagship arrived at the German shipyard on 27th October 1986 and the carefully planned work began immediately.

The first major job was to strip out the boilers, turbines and other redundant machinery. This was done by removing the funnel and using the emptied shaft below as a passageway - both for removing scrap material and installing the new machinery.

Great care was taken in the removal of the old equipment and, because of the presence of asbestos in the insulation, a delay in the work was caused. This was undesirable as Lloyd Werft were liable to pay penalties for any delays by the day.

Eckart Knoth, chairman of Lloyd Werft, described the stripping-out process as being 'like hell'. By the time it was complete 4,700 tons of scrapped turbines, boilers, pipes and other broken organs of the *Queen* lay on the quayside, dominated by the comparatively still pristine - but to be modified - funnel.

The emptied machinery spaces appeared cavernous with heavy-lift trucks being dwarfed by the surroundings in which they now incongruously moved.

When the liner was being built in Scotland, twenty years previously, a scale model of the engine room had been made to show the location of each and every piece of equipment and pipe.

Looking very forlorn the *Queen* sits in the Kaiserdock II dry dock, Bremerhaven, whilst her engine room, interior, propellers and new penthouse suites are gutted, refurbished and fitted. The P & O liner *Canberra* came in during the *QE2's* stay for a refit, although less extensive, of her own.

Lloyd Werft, Bremerhaven

Similarly, now, a model was made of the new layout and many problems were ironed out well beforehand.

The first major items of machinery to be installed were the British-made electric propulsion motors, shipped to Germany in sections and reassembled at the shipyard, which were carefully lowered through the temporary hatchway and slid aft.

A large floating crane, HEBE 2, performed all the heavy lifting tasks, her lifting capacity of 750 tons being more than adequate for the weights of the *QE2's* machinery.

Then came the nine, four-stroke, nine cylinder diesel engines which were also lowered and slid into place on their seatings in the ultimately unmanned engine rooms.

One of the mini MAN-B&W 9L 58/64 diesel engines on its test bed in Augsburg.

MAN-B&W

A complete electrical generator shown prior to its packing and shipment to Germany.

GEC Turbine Generators Limited

Top: Reappearing slightly 'thickened about the waist' after her major 1987 refit, the *QE2* was ready for her third decade in service.
Cedric Wasser

Left: The Queen's Room as it appeared in 1987. The original chairs which had reflected the trumpet-like columns have been replaced by cubic armchairs in soft, brown leather, perhaps less pleasing to the eye than their predecessors. *Cunard*

Below left: The refurbished swimming pool on One Deck Lido boasts a vivid Cunard lion in mosaic tiles. *Cunard*

Below right: The refurbished spectacular Columbia Restaurant with its 750 seat capacity. *Cunard*

Top: The Double Down Room was one of the public rooms to be dramatically altered in the 1987 refit and was renamed the Grand Lounge. The old stainless steel stairway has gone (the new one is sited at the opposite end of the room) and shops have encroached even further into the upper (Double Up) lounge area. *Cunard*

Centre left: A white piano with a glass top and surrounding glass bar provided the focal point in the new (1987) Yacht Club bar (ex Double Down Bar) on the Upper Deck. *Cunard*

Centre right: This view illustrates the plush conditions in the cabins that awaited first class passengers. *Cunard*

Right: The corridor of the new suites fitted in Bremerhaven by Lloyd Werft. This view was generally only seen by those few privileged to travel in this exclusive accommodation. *Cunard*

The nine engines, MAN-B&W L58/64 (ie, the cylinders were 580 millimetres in diameter and the pistons moved through a 640 millimetre stroke) were named Alpha, Bravo, Charlie etc. up to number 9 which was India.

Part of the contract stipulated that the liner should achieve 28.5 knots on 85% of the engine power and that there should be no increase in vibration over that induced by the now displaced machinery.

To overcome any vibration problem the engines were mounted on layered rubber resilient mounts, placed at an angle to the engine seats, which would keep vibration to an absolute minimum.

With her old, smooth-running steam turbines the *QE2* , at 28.5 knots, had used six hundred tons of oil fuel a day, thus burning up 120,000 tons per year (at £100 per ton). With her new engines consumption would hopefully be reduced to 270 tons a day.

The waste heat from the machinery would also be put to good use. It would be utilised to heat accommodation, to pre-heat the thick oil fuel, provide steam to the various hotel services and help to produce one thousand tons of fresh water a day from the sea via four Serck vacuum evaporators. Another 450 tons per day would be produced from the sea by Reverse Osmosis Plant equipment that had also provided additional fresh water on the Falklands 'cruise'.

The ability to produce more than enough fresh water would enable the liner to reduce her fresh water tankage by 40%.

At the 'business end' of all the propulsion machinery were the two propellers which had to absorb the enormous power produced by the nine diesels.

The QE2 has always remained the largest, most powerful twin screw vessel in the world. Stone Manganese Marine, the manufacturers of her original six (fixed) bladed, 5791 millimetre diameter propellers had insisted that 110000 shp was the maximum that two propellers could absorb.

Now 130,000 shp was required to be absorbed and the Dutch firm of LIPS, of Drunen, had designed propellers with five blades each. But these blades were controllable, they could be turned remotely on their bosses. This meant that the special astern machinery that was required with fixed blade propellers could be dispensed with as, by turning the controlled blades sufficiently, the liner could be halted and then sent astern whilst the propellers still rotated in the same direction.

The propellers would also be operated at only two speeds - 144 revolutions per minute for speeds above 18 knots and 72 revolutions for those below. The controlled pitch of the blades would do the rest, enabling the liner to go from 34 knots ahead to 19 knots astern.

The propeller blades were also 'skewed' - scimitar shaped - to cut down the effects of cavitation and to reduce the propeller induced vibration on the hull.

The new 5,800 millimetre diameter propellers were to be augmented by recently developed (but long theorised) pseudo-propellers called Grim wheels (named after their professor inventor). At 6.7 metres diameter they were larger than the propellers, had seven slender uniquely shaped blades (or vanes) and freely rotated at about one third of the CPPs' speed.

Their purpose was to absorb the waste thrust lost from the propellers. This was absorbed by the turbine like inner part of the vane and converted into thrust by the vane tip which thus acted like a second propeller. A worthwhile increase in efficiency of almost 4% was expected by the use of these wheels.

The old 32 ton, manganese bronze propellers were sold off. One would be retained as a dockland exhibit in England but its partner was scheduled to become the basis of two and a half thousand sets of high quality golf clubs!

Whilst the *Queen Elizabeth 2* was having a new heart installed into her very depths the shipyard was also restyling much of her accommodation, both passenger and crew. A study of the deck plans contained within this book will indicate the changes that have been made in these areas between the liner's building and major conversion in 1987.

The manning of the liner would also change under Cunard's new plans. The all British crew were given the chance of either contracting their labour or else accept a 'golden handshake' and hand their jobs over to other, perhaps foreign,

Shipshape once again the engine room is ready for business!
Cunard

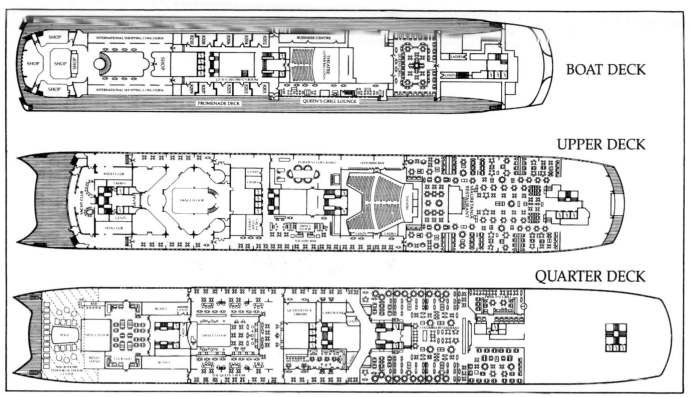

The main passenger decks as they appeared after their 1987 re-arrangement. It is interesting to compare these layouts with those from the time when the 963 foot long liner was built (see inside back cover).   *Cunard*

contractors. In spite of union protests that the men would be selling British jobs of which they were only 'temporary custodians', the liner now boasts a multi-national crew in line with other major cruise liners.

Suffice it to say that the whole conversion cost Cunard in excess of £92million, a price that was much cheaper than building an equivalent new ship. Of the cost £2 million alone went to restyling the Tables of the World - originally the Britannia - restaurant. Renamed in honour of the *Mauretania* (Cunard's venerable, record breaking and most loved liner of 1907) the restaurant displays an oversize painting of that liner leaving the shipyard as well as beautifully framed photographs taken on board and of her building and a magnificent model of the old four funnelled liner stands in a glass case for all to admire.

After an absence of many years in an ocean liner restaurant dancing has been re-introduced with the provision of dance floor facilities in both Columbia (another early Cunard transatlantic paddlesteamer) and Mauretania restaurants.

With the expenditure of 1,700,000 man-hours the biggest merchantship conversion ever undertaken was almost complete.

Trials had to be run in the North Sea to test the unification of the whole. These lasted from April 8th until the 22nd. Fuel consumption was as hoped for as were the speeds attained. The maximum speed achieved of 33.8 knots left many, including Cunard (in spite of historical precedents), wondering whether the liner would now contend for the legendary Blue Ribband still held by the American liner *United Stated*.

Testing the new power plant had taken the ship, travelling at full speed, 3 minutes 38 seconds to come to a halt in just over a mile! A further twelve minutes and she was going astern at 19 knots!

Vibration, too, was measurably down in the public rooms although it remained at a similar level as before in the aft sections of the ship.

Work continued during the trials in the hotel areas of the ship in an attempt to finish the uncompleted tasks before the liner left the shipyard. In spite of the frantic efforts workmen would travel with the ship to New York in an attempt to clear the backlog of unfinished work that still needed to be completed in cabins and to plumbing and air conditioning.

The shipyard handed over the *QE2* to her owners on 25th April during a ceremony held on board. Eckart Knoth (chairman), Dieter Haake (managing director) and Werner Luken (project manager for the *QE2*) represented Lloyd Werft whilst Cunard's Ralph Bahna (president and managing director), Alan Kennedy (chairman) and project manager, Mike Novak - not to mention Captain Lawrence Portet - could look on a difficult job well done. The project had not been without its heartaches and moments of apprehension but the company was glad to have its ship back in good order, retrieved from the mess, noise and disorder that degrades the loveliest of ships when in shipyard hands.

Sir Nigel Broackes, chairman of Trafalgar House, was also present at the ceremony amongst the five hundred distinguished guests. He had hosted a party on board the evening before.

Lloyd Werft presented the *QE2* with a special gift - a large, embossed leather marinescape that had originally hung in the First Class Smoking Room of the four funnelled, German record breaker *Kaiser Wilhelm der Grosse* of 1897.

For their part Cunard presented a cheque to the shipyard's welfare fund. In appreciation of the business that the shipping line had brought to his city, the Mayor of Bremerhaven gave a mahogany boxed compass to a smiling Ralph Bahna.

At last the time came for the liner to leave the shipyard that had instilled her with an invigorated hope for the future. She carried with her on her trip across the North Sea many special guests - and also several hundred shipyard workers frantically trying to finish those jobs which were left uncompleted in order to get the ship away from the shipyard in time.

Above: In mid-July 1987 the *QE2* enters the King Geroge V dry dock in Southampton to have the remaining vanes cut off the Grim wheel bosses.
Roger Hardingham

Below: One of the propeller bosses with remains of the grim wheels still attached is lifted away from the ship.

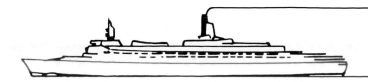

Chapter Twelve

A Second Career

The *Queen Elizabeth 2's* re-entry into service as almost a new ship called for a special, singular honour - a second maiden voyage - and the first day of the revitalised commercial life of the *QE2*, Wednesday 29th April, 1987, started in a most auspicious way.

The Cunard had arranged for several hundred of Southampton's most deserving children to board the ship to make a short commemorative trip down Southampton Water to an anchorage in the confines of The Solent that lay between the Hampshire coast and the northern shores of the Isle of Wight.

There a special guest, Her Royal Highness Diana, Princess of Wales, would join the liner arriving by launch from the yachting town of Cowes on the nearby island. She then travelled with the children on their return journey to Southampton, chatting with many of them *en-route*. The wooded shores of Hampshire and its New Forest must have slipped by the ship almost unnoticed.

The *en-fête* vessel was over-flown by two Harrier Jump Jets of the Royal Air Force and, on reaching the River Test where she would berth alongside the Queen Elizabeth II Terminal, the *Queen Elizabeth 2* was greeted by her contemporary co-masterpiece of British engineering, the supersonic Concorde. The delta winged aircraft saluted in its fly-past both the magnificent ship below and those on board her. Both liner and aircraft had co-operated on many an occasion in symbiotic ventures bringing together the offer of a dream-voyage of a lifetime to those wishing to commemorate, perhaps, a special event with a spectacular journey.

After the children had disembarked the ship was prepared in readiness to embark the passengers and their luggage in readiness for the liners departure on her "Second Maiden Voyage". Just after seven o'clock in the chill of a late April evening the liner motored (for she was no longer a steamship) down Southampton Water being passed, as on many occasions before, by one of the red and white hydrofoils that operate between Southampton and the Isle of Wight. During this and subsequent immediate post-refit voyages - and as is usually expected on a "new" ships entry into service - teething troubles were experienced due, to a great extent, to a modern insistence that a ships essential husbandry and maintenance should be kept subservient to the "bottom line" of a balance sheet. But because this particular sailing had been surrounded by so much publicity, the ship had to sail - ready internally or not.

To mark the final days of the *QE2* as a steamship several ex-skippers met on board. Included in this picture are Captain 'Bil' Warwick (right), Mortimer Hehir, Peter Jackson and Bob Arnott (third, fourth and fifth from right).   *Southern Newspapers*

In the lower swinging ground off the QEII Terminal the *Queen Elizabeth 2*, assisted by tugs, arrives from Bremehaven in 1987. The two large tenders aft on her boat deck would later be removed.

R. Bruce-Grice

Caught up in the resultant dilemma several passengers had justifiable cause to complain during the *Queen's* first few inaugural voyages. Plumbing problems (including floods, strange happenings in toilets as well as showers not functioning); air-conditioning failing in public rooms; uncontrollable heating and even water that dripped onto diners in the prestigious Queen's Grill. The unfinished state of some staterooms and the inexperience of an almost new hotel staff led to many a passenger voicing disquiet. Compensations were subsequently paid to both passengers and crew for the discomforts experienced in all affected areas.

On a cruise to Madeira and Tenerife following the second maiden voyage two hundred passengers had their bookings cancelled. These passengers had paid for accommodation on 5-Deck but the restructuring of this deck was still mostly incomplete and those cabins that were available had been allocated to workmen embarked to complete the unfinished work remaining from the major refit. The resultant refunds and compensation were costly, Cunard paying out around £100,000 as a result.

The new propulsion machinery deep within the ship was also not without its problems. During an early post-refit cruise (Southampton depart 20th July 1987, six days from £590) she limped into Gibraltar on only one propeller. As part of the ensuing repairs a half-ton electrical coil had to be

flown out to "Gib" from the UK for fitting to one of the main electrical generators. One of the scheduled subsequent Portugese ports of call, at Praia da Rocha on the Algarve, had to be cancelled as the *QE2* sailed back to Southampton, where she arrived one day late at a mere 18 knots. However, according to Cunard, the passengers had enjoyed their extra, albeit enforced, day at sea.

But, as on previous occasions - as well as on occasions yet to come - the complaints were fortunately overcome by results and receded into a memory of past regrets as the liner resettled into her annual round of cruises and line voyages.

Soon, Douglas Ward, author of the respected "Berlitz Complete Handbook to Cruising" and editor of "Cruise Digest Reports", was able to summarise the contemporary impact of the renovated liner: "*QE2* is now the most perfectly integrated passenger ship afloat. She has no equal - for no other ship can cross the Atlantic like the *Queen* - or provide such facilities and style for cruising."

"She is, quite simply, the worlds finest ship and the last of the true express ocean liners."

"Without doubt, the most magnificent ship in the world. And very, very British."

The "Britishness" of the *QE2* had gradually become recognized as one of her most saleable assets - even considering that a proportion of her crewing had been given over to non-British staff. Not only was prestigious

Britishness for sale but Cunard were beginning to realise that the nostalgic style of the old liners also had a marketable value but over the next few years art-deco - the "Ocean Liner" style of the 1930s - and the history of the Cunard Line itself began to make a well-received appearance on board during various refits.

In 1986, as previously mentioned, the British aspect of the liner was in danger of being lost forever. In order to run the vessel in an increasingly competitive market Cunard had to run its flagship in an equally competitive way. Accordingly, this meant employing crew at relative rates and therefore the company had to review its crewing policies. The "new" image of the liner after her major refit provided such an opportunity for such changes of personnel.

Consequently, the British hotel staff found that they had a fight on their hands. The National Union of Seamen became involved and at a meeting of its QE2 members in Southampton, under the chairmanship of Sam McCluskie and with the parliamentary representation of John Prescott (himself an ex-Cunarder and NUS official), the 800 crew members voted for their future. The ballot was carried at about 600 to 50 in favour of accepting Cunard's terms with 130 members declining to vote on advice from the NUS. This pay-off represented a "golden handshake" of one years salary per man plus £900 for each year of service. In some individual cases payments of £40,000 were made and would, in total, cost Cunard a total in excess of £14-million.

Under the new manning arrangements around forty different nationalities became employed on the ship, although the majority of crew remained British, sub-contracting their labour through staffing agencies such as the Columbia Ship Management of Cyprus. But the ship had been "de-unionised", reportedly resulting in a greater flexibility in working hours. As an added spin-off it was also felt that the ship was being run to a higher standard and was actually a happier ship once the changes had been made and accepted and, at a later date, when the technical departments - the engine and deck departments - followed suit, the QE2 became a better ship than ever with resultant increases in the quality of maintenance both externally as well as internally.

During the height of the industrial unrest, Cunard threatened to move the liners home port from Southampton, possibly to a new terminal in Cherbourg. Fortunately, this plan dissolved as the discontent subsided and the new working arrangements became implemented.

However, before her next cruise to Lisbon departing on May 30th, the Queen undertook one transatlantic "cruise" (the current euphemism for the traditional transatlantic line voyage) with each leg of the twelve day voyage taking six days (four complete days and five nights at sea). The eastbound trip proved, however, to be more than could be expected at that time of year as an unpleasant surprise lay in wait for the Queen Elizabeth 2. One of the worst storms encountered by the vessel at that season hit the ship with forty-foot waves driven by winds of fifty miles an hour. The liner was battered for more than fifteen hours during which time the passengers were advised to remain in their cabins. Amongst the £50,000 of damage caused during the ordeal four windows high upon the vessel had been broken by the heavy seas and two grand pianos had been destroyed. The ship arrived in Southampton several hours behind schedule.

Top: The elegant lines of classical design in the *QE2* are demonstrated in this study of the gently curving steel front of her Bridge set against the straight lines of wood decking and distant horizon, all accentuated by the contrast of light and shade. *Cunard*

Left: A striking view of QE2 from the air as she cruises past the Needles, Isle of Wight, *en route* to the Atlantic.

Two transatlantics followed a West Indies cruise that had terminated in New York on 4th July. In between each transatlantic the *QE2* was dry-docked in the mighty King George V Graving Dock (originally built for the fabled *Queen Mary*) in Southampton. During her 30-hour overnight stay in the dock (9th-10th July) the remains of the Grim Wheels were removed and replaced by conventional propeller cones. The stubs of these "wheels" had originally comprised seven vanes mounted on a central hub, carefully designed to absorb some of the thrust lost from the controllable pitch propellers that had replaced the vessels 1969 - designed fixed-pitched propellers. Increased speeds - with a slight hope of taking the prestigious Blue Ribband of the North Atlantic - and efficiencies in saving up to £1,000 per day in the fuel bill had eagerly been anticipated at the time of fitting and during the trials that followed. On removal the vanes stubs were retained for analysis by metallurgists from Messrs. Lips. A later offer by these manufacturers to replace the Wheels would be declined by Cunard's technical staff.

Whilst still in place the Grim Wheel stubs had adversely affected the comfort of the crew and of passengers berthed aft by creating vibration and the CPP propellers, which had been designed to run with the Grims, did not alleviate the vibration experienced after the stubs removal to any noticeable extent. Consequently, twelve passenger cabins would remain untenable until a new set of propellers could be designed, manufactured and fitted.

Because of the dry-docking *QE2* missed her 11.30am sailing on 10th July by a few hours but she was able to make up this lost time and returned to schedule by reducing the time of her next turn-around in Southampton (that proceeded her cruise to Gibraltar) to a mere six hours.

August saw the retirement of Captain Lawrence Portet, a tall but private man, who had seen the liners transition from steamship to motorship. His place as Senior Captain was taken by Captain Alan Bennell, a dashing, gregarious man who would prove to be very popular with both crew and passengers. Above all, his love for the ship now under his command was evident to those with whom he came in contact.

A new era had definitely started in the career of *Queen Elizabeth 2*.

The *QE2* glides between the Isle of Wight (with Cowes in the distance) and the Hampshire shore at Stokes Bay near Gosport in the foreground. There are many photographic opportunities in the approaches to Southampton Water. *Author*

Chapter Thirteen

Propellers to the Fore!

The end of 1987 also saw the end of one of the old propellers that had been removed during the *QE2's* big refit. Of the original, 19-foot diameter, six-bladed design, the 32 ton propellers had been purchased by Messrs. Sandhill (Bullion) Ltd., of Leeds who planned to cut one of them into manageable pieces within Southampton docks prior to transporting the scrap to the Birkenhead factory of Stone Manganese (the propellers had been fashioned in their London works) for smelting. The resultant smaller, cast ingots would then be taken to St. Andrews, the Mecca of British golf, where they would be formed into 750 sets of golf clubs that would be available to American, European and Japanese golfers at around £700 to £1,000 per set. The second propeller would last until mid-1990 when it would be taken, whole, to St. Andrews where it was put on display during the British Open Golf Championship. Afterwards it followed the same fate as its twin being transformed by Messrs. Sandhill Swilken of St. Andrews into the "Q2 Putter Royale", later sold for £170 each (Duty Free!) on board the liner.

Before the old year was out the *Queen* made a pre-Christmas sunshine cruise to West Africa calling in at Lisbon, Gibraltar, Tenerife, Dakar in Senegal, the Cape Verde Islands and Madeira prior to returning to Southampton on 12th December.

Arriving at Tenerife on 3rd December during this cruise the *Queen* decided to make her mark - or rather Tenerife made its mark on the *Queen!* - as, whilst entering Santa Cruz, she came in rather too quickly and bumped the quay wall, buckling one of her hull plates to a depth of nine inches. Delayed in the port for 24 hours a temporary replacement plate was patched over the damaged area before the ship continued with her cruise. A permanent repair would be made during her August 1988 refit in Germany.

The *Queen Elizabeth 2's* first major sortie as a motorship came during what was billed as "The 1988 Maiden Voyage Across the World", but in effect took her from New York (departing 13th January, 1988) through the Panama Canal to destinations in and around the Pacific and Indian Oceans.

Calls were made at Fort Lauderdale, Acapulco, Los Angeles, at various islands in the South Pacific and ports in New Zealand and Australia where the ship became officially involved with the latter's Bicentennial celebrations. Then it was on to islands in the Indian Ocean, through to East Africa before heading eastwards to Southeast Asia and Hong Kong. Up to here various shorter segments of the cruise had been

advertised as being available to those other than the full cruise passengers but from Hong Kong to China, Japan, north Pacific islands and back to LA prior to visiting destinations in the Caribbean, it would appear from the itinerary that only the full voyage passengers were embarked until the liner reached Fort Lauderdale where fly-cruise passengers once again joined her. The *QE2* arrived back in New York on 29th April.

It was whilst the ship was cruising the islands of the South Pacific that an announcement was made that the liner would be chartered in 1989 by a group of Japanese businessmen in a deal eventually to be worth almost £20-million to Cunard. Lasting for a staggering 72 days the ship would be moored at Yokohama as an important part of that citys 150th Anniversary celebrations being used for commercial exhibitions and conferences as well as for hotel purposes. The Japanese ranked amongst the greatest admirers of the great ship, ranking her in their affections for all things that reflected the best in British quality.

The 32-day round South America cruise that had been scheduled for the period now to be taken up by the forthcoming charter was cancelled as were various shorter cruises planned for the Los Angeles/Pacific area.

Towards the end of the Pacific and Indian Ocean cruise in late April, a further enquiry was received, again by the ardent Japanese, concerning a second, even longer charter. This time the city of Osaka wanted the ship for a six months charter for use as part of that citys planned World Exposition in 1989. A fee of £50-million was rumoured.

The admiration of the Japanese for the *QE2* was being translated into healthy returns for the Cunard.

Meanwhile, the *Queen Elizabeth 2* arrived in Southampton at 5pm on 4th May for a rare overnight stay. Before she sailed on the 5th an unusual press call was

In a shower of flame and flying sparks from a burner's torch one of the discarded propellers is cut into pieces ready for the furnace and ultimate transformation into sets of unique golf clubs.
Southern Newspapers

organised by the British Post Office. A special 26-pence postage stamp had been produced commemorating the fiftieth anniversary of the launch of the *QE2*'s namesake, the legendary 83,676 gross ton *Queen Elizabeth* - the "Old Lizzie" as she had been affectionately known to decades of crew and travellers.

To launch the new stamp Relief Captain Robin Woodall, along with British television personality Jimmy Saville (a devoted *QE2* fan and traveller) and retired Cunard Commodore Geoffrey Marr (one-time captain of the *Queen Elizabeth*) stood around on the cold, windswept quayside waiting for the press to complete their work. Both elderly and infirm on his legs, Commodore Marr found the experience to be particularly gruelling.

30th June saw the *Queen* arriving in Southampton with a most unusual item on her manifest. In her hold she carried a steel coffin which contained the remains of renowned Hungarian-born composer Bela Bartok, writer of such atonal compositions as "Bluebeard's Castle" and "Music For Strings, Percussion and Celesta". Having emigrated to the United States in 1940 he was being returned to his beloved city of Budapest for a state funeral 43 years after his death.

Otherwise the summer season progressed uneventfully for the *QE2* until it was time for an unscheduled overhaul. This took place in Germany where she arrived on 1st August after an incredible four-and-a-half hour turnaround in Southampton, a ten day transatlantic having been cancelled to enable the work to be done. Amongst the work to be undertaken was the replacement of the hull plate previously damaged in Tenerife, the overhaul of the ships stabilisers and the removal of the controllable pitch propellers that had been designed to work with the deposed Grim Wheels and which were now, as a consequence, out of balance. The replacement propellers (also controllable pitch and provided under the terms of the Grim Wheel guarantee by Lips) would hopefully alleviate the vibration problems that had been plaguing the after end of the ship ever since the disintegration of the revolutionary, vaned appendages.

The hope for the new propellers proved to be well-founded as, when the ship was sent on her post-refit trials, the crew asked why their ship was apparently going so slowly. One can only imagine Captain Bennell's amusement when he told his men that the *QE2* had been achieving 31 knots! The lack of the vibration so accustomed to over the past few months had lulled the men into a false sense of speed! Captain Bennell later told reporters that the Bremerhaven trip had also been used by the SAS to practice their specialist units expertise in overcoming maritime hijackers.

September, 1988, brought yet another accolade to the *Queen Elizabeth 2* when she achieved her two-millionth mile, doing so in half the time that the old *Queen Elizabeth* had taken.

It was also in September that retired Commodore Geoffrey Marr was invited to sail on the ship in order to talk to the passengers about his time in command of the *Queen Elizabeth* and of the time that he was with her in an advisory capacity during her last voyage when she had been renamed *Seawise University*. As such she had been taken from her interrupted retirement in Fort Lauderdale, Florida, to Hong Kong where, during the last days of her conversion to a floating university, she had caught fire and capsized - completely destroyed.

However, the Commodore decided that he was now too infirm to make the special trip to New York that would celebrate the fiftieth anniversary of the launch of his beloved *Queen Elizabeth* that had occurred on 27th September, 1938. Besides, he said, he wanted his old passengers to remember him as he had been - strolling the decks with his greatcoat swirling about him - and not as an old man.

In his stead the current author was invited to speak and the trip, Voyage 682, departing from Southampton on 29th September, proved to be a memorable one not only for the commemorative events that were scheduled to take place on board but also for the surprise unscheduled events that were added onto the crossing - courtesy of Nature.

These started as the sea became steadily unsettled during the evening of the second day out until a Force 8 to 9 gale, the first of two such gales encountered in the course of the voyage, gave the ship a heavy pitch as she ploughed westwards.

A visit to the Bridge during the late evening of the first storm showed the huge waves, phosphorescent in the faint light of the ship, breaking either side of the plunging bow before, broken into huge clouds of spray, the seas cascaded aft towards the Bridge front where built-in wind deflectors took the spray vertically up behind the Bridge wings, creating dimly illuminated ghostly green curtains. Within the cabins the movement of the ship was also felt as the ship slowly and steadily rolled to either

Captain Robin Woodall (left), retired Cunard Commodore Geoffrey Marr (right) and an as always exuberant Jimmy Saville help to launch a postage stamp bearing an image of the never-to-be-forgotten *Queen Elizabeth*.

Southern Newspapers

side, each roll being checked with a slight judder as the stabilisers took charge and corrected the liners' sideways motion. The thinly veneered panels lining the cabin's bulkheads gently creaked with each movement.

Two such storms should have been enough for one crossing of the Atlantic. On the fourth day out an announcement, broadcast during breakfast, advised the passengers that the *QE2* was approaching the Grand Banks (off Newfoundland, Nova Scotia) and that aquatic and airborne wildlife could possibly be seen as might a few fishing boats but, as the ship was .."well South of the normal ice area...", there was no chance of any ice being encountered.

A mid-morning visit to the Bridge was made, during which dolphins and a herd of Right whales were seen along to starboard, was interrupted by the author's wife: "What's that white thing on the horizon?"

"Probably a fishing boat, madam."

"Looks too white to be a fishing boat to me - looks more like ice."

At this binoculars were raised -- "My God! It is ice! Call the Captain!"

Captain Bennell soon made his appearance and was transfixed by the first ice that he had seen on the Atlantic for thirty years - and which the radar had failed to detect - on the horizon. He made an announcement over the ship's broadcast system and, as passengers flocked to the Boat Deck rails, said mischievously "I bet that's mucked up a few lectures!"

Changing course the *Queen Elizabeth 2* was navigated to within half a mile of the iceberg and, even at that distance, the cold emanating from its mass could be felt. A bank of mist surmounting its peak slowly undulated and, in doing so, gave the appearance that the berg was continuously changing shape. The swell of the sea around the base of the iceberg was eerily discoloured a pale green, illuminated by the light that was reflected from the submerged bulk of the 'berg.

Soon, the ice was receding astern and the excitement was over as the liner resumed her course. On the next voyage Captain Bennell would take his ship towards the by-now well-charted, slow-moving iceberg to show it off to his passengers. From the time that it was seen it was nick-named by the officers on the Bridge as "Benny's Berg" in honour of their Captain!

Much of this particular voyage was being recorded by a publishers photographer, Ian Burney, and his pictures would appear in a book co-authored by the ships First Officer, Peter Moxom. Their combined effort, "From the Bridge - QE2 Cunard's Flagship", would provide a fascinating account of the internal workings and organisation of the ship. The captions to some of the photographs gave rise to concern in high places as, although they reflected the banter that occurs in many a workplace, they were perhaps unsuitable for publication!

The last quarter of 1988 seemed to be intermittently plagued with high winds. On 6th October, when sailing from Southampton at the outset of a nine-day cruise to Ibiza, Cannes, Barcelona, Gibraltar, and Lisbon (nine days from £925) the *Queen* was caught by winds gusting up to 72mph. She had just rounded the long finger of Calshot Spit that, with its ancient castle built in the time of Henry VIII to protect the entrance to Southampton Water, juts out from the New Forest and separates Southampton Water from The Solent where, after making the turn to port to go around the submerged Brambles Bank, the wind caught the ship and pushed her bow to starboard towards the Lepe shore.

After her 1999 refit - and after the debut of the blockbuster movie 'Titanic' - the *Queen* was given traditional wooden deck chairs on which pampered passengers could soak up both sun and sea air.

Author

Because of the apparent risk and as an inward bound containership, the 50,000 ton *Benavon*, was also in the area Captain Bennell ordered the ship to go astern to avoid running out of the channel. With her new engines responding immediately, the liner went astern at 8 knots until she had recovered her position and then everything continued as normal. The event received what was considered to be unwarranted coverage by the press and reports of "...a near collision.." were unfounded.

Most of November was spent cruising the Caribbean with Captain Woodall in command, sailing the waters that he had recently left after having spent ten years there, to join the *Queen Elizabeth 2* as Relief Captain.

Although due to return to New York the liner made one of her intermittent diversions to Boston, Massachusetts, and it was from here that she sailed on the night of 21st November, heading for Southampton.

Captain Woodall recalled that a NNW gale Force 8 was blowing as the ship sailed from the New England port and that this wind had increased to Force 9 on the 22nd. The wind then veered round to WNW the next day, increasing to Force 10 with a big sea running. The direction of the ship was changed on occasion to make it slightly easier for the passengers as she was producing some nasty rolls. After a couple of days the wind went round to the South so, for a while, the ship was ahead of the wind and it was a little more comfortable.

However, two days later the wind direction changed yet again, this time coming over the bow from an East by South direction. The ship had to slow down again to 9 knots and was thus thirty hours late in arriving in Southampton. Another damaged piano, broken crockery, buckled rails on the foc'sle and scattered furniture were some of the "victims" of the four day storm. At the storms height the sound of it could be heard over the ship-to-shore radio in the United Kingdom!

Captain Woodall would later say that, although it was a very nasty storm, worse ones were later to be experienced, confirming his own suspicions that the weather is changing on the North Atlantic with both stronger winds and seas bigger than encountered before.

A cruise to West Africa and the Atlantic isles was followed by a short, four day jaunt from 11th to 14th December around the English Channel calling in at Cherbourg, hopefully creating a taste for a longer cruise to many of those on board.

Arrival back in Southampton, 14th December, meant the arrival of a very special visitor. Her Majesty Queen Elizabeth, the Queen Mother, boarded the liner along with three hundred other specially invited guests including retired Commodores Donald McLean and Geoffrey Marr and Captain John Treasure Jones. The royal visit brought to a head the celebrations that had been held to commemorate the launching of the *Queen Elizabeth* that Her Majesty had named and christened in 1938.

In her speech about the old ship that had borne her name, the Queen Mother said :

"....Throughout the years that followed the *Queen Elizabeth* was a symbol of so much pride in our country."

"...For me and for many who travelled in her it was a sad day in November 1968 when the *Queen Elizabeth* sailed from Southampton for the last time, leaving a legacy of memories."

She continued: "I am sure it is a name that will live on in history, just like *Golden Hind*, *Victory* and *Cutty Sark*."

Her Majesty then made reference to the ship in which she now spoke: "Like her predecessor the *Queen Elizabeth 2* is a fine ambassador for this country."

The *QE2* spent Christmas in the Caribbean with Christmas Day in Barbados and New Years Day in Fort Lauderdale. A shorter cruise in the same waters followed that ended in New York on 13th January, 1989.

During her Pacific cruise at the beginning of March the *Queen* was buffeted by a severe storm with forty foot waves that lasted for six hours as she sailed between Tahiti and New Zealand. As damage occured to both ship and those on board (forty one passengers and crew had suffered minor injuries) Captain Bennell was furious that he had not been told of these adverse conditions, which with sufficient warning, could have been avoided by prudent navigation. The New Zealand weather bureau later said that their lack of warning was indicative of governmental cut-backs in their service.

It was then time for the first of the two Japanese charters that would take place that year.

A *Queen Mary* anniversary on board saw many retired Cunard captains return to their old command. Left to right (standing) Commodore Douglas Ridley, current Captain Laurence Portet and Captain Bob Arnott. Seated (l to r) Captains John Treasure Jones, 'Bil' Warwick, William Law and Mortimer Heier. Having retired with his beloved *Queen Mary*, Captain Jones was the only captain present not to have been master of the QE2.

Southern Newspapers

Chapter Fourteen

Anniversaries and Accolades

1989 was to prove to be an important and profitable year for the Cunard.

The first of the Japanese charters took the *Queen Elizabeth 2* to the city of Yokohama which was celebrating its 130th Anniversary in which the *Queen* was to play an important part. Commencing 27th March the ship would remain berthed alongside her pier at the citys passenger terminal.

A consortium of Japanese companies had chartered the ship for £250,000 a day and it was hoped that this money would be recouped by using the ship as an hotel at £1,690 a night for a suite and for companies to use her for corporate entertaining at £600,000 per day. Both hotel and corporate bookings were eventually well below those estimated. A charge was made to those just wanting to look over the vessel (on-board sales figures exceeded the estimate) and a smaller fee was levied on those thousands just wanting to walk alongside her on the quayside to look at the ship that they considered to be an icon of British quality! Signs and staff on board were changed to Japanese for the term of the charter.

The liner was also licensed for weddings and twenty couples decided to take advantage of this opportunity although the Captain did not perform the ceremonies! The ship's shops and facilities were all open and a programme of entertainments kept the visitors amused. But, in spite of the report that 69,000 Japanese had stayed on board and that 180,000 people had made day visits (at almost £60 for three hours, including lunch) to the ship, the charter still made a loss for the charterers but it was considered to be part of a "learning curve". If the venture had not completely been a commercial success for the Japanese it certainly had been one in an operational sense.

Captain Woodall later said that Cunard had learnt a lot about the Japanese and that they, in turn, had learnt a lot on how to run a big ship. It all ended with both sides respecting each other socially as well as commercially.

Both the Captain and his wife had thoroughly enjoyed themselves on their day sorties from the ship: "The Japanese people were terribly kind and awfully helpful - they couldn't do enough for us - and generous to a fault."

"Wherever my wife and I went we were recognised because we had been on television...and being 6 foot 4

The long, sleek bow of the *Queen Elizabeth 2* is seen to advantage in this dockside shot at Southampton.   *Peter Seden*

inches and a Westerner in Japan makes one stand out to a certain extent! ....People would come up and talk to us - total strangers - just to ask about the ship and our life on board."

The Captain's overiding impression of Japan ("...a fascinating country...") - "Traffic jams!!..There's an awful lot of cars in an awful small space!"

After seventy-two days in Yokohama the *Queen Elizabeth 2* sailed on 4th June and returned to Southampton, where she arrived at the beginning of July.

Once home, it would not be long before the *QE2* was again making national headlines - but this time they were of the scandal-making variety.

Environmental issues were rightly becoming a concern of major international importance and any infringement brought forth the wrath of nations upon the perpertrators head. In this instance it was the unfortunate lot of the *QE2* to be caught, literally in the act!

Provision had been made on the liner in her early days to dump bagged rubbish over the side but, with the adaption of garbage compressors and the introduction of legislation to protect the seas of the world and its wildlife, this practice was rightly no longer acceptable, unless the waste had been rendered into an an easily dispersable bio-degradable slurry prior to disposal.

A damning video was made by two young crew members whilst in the Caribbean in late June showing other crew members dumping black plastic bags of garbage over the stern under the cover of darkness and the video was sent to a national newspaper.

Captain Bennell later explained that the ship had had several thousands of pounds spent in upgrading her garbage disposal by using environmentally friendly methods and that the release of the video was the first he had heard of the illicit dumping.

October brought two items of satisfying news for Cunard and Trafalgar House. Firstly the Round Britain Cruise that would preceed the celebrations commemorating the 150th Anniversary of the Cunard Line in 1990 was sold out and, secondly, it was disclosed that the new diesel-electric propulsion system was using one-third less oil-fuel and, as a result, was saving the company around £7-million a year in fuel bills!

In November, prior to her second charter in Japan, the *Queen Elizabeth 2* was given a short refit in Southampton, a rare occurence in recent years. Work included surveys on boilers and structure; machinery overhauls; overhauling lifeboats and checks on other lifesaving equipment; and refurbishing passenger areas and accommodation that included new carpets and upholstery.

The *Queen* was passed to the charter group just before Christmas on her arrival in Honolulu and ultimately arrived in Osaka on 28th December at the outset of an incredible 180-day stay. During this time she would perform similar functions to those that she performed in Yokohama but would also make ten short cruises as part of her itininary. She would be in Japan during the Spring - an important time in that country - and would be an essential part of World Exposition 1990. A similar fee to that received in Yokohama, £250,000 a day, was being paid for the charter, netting nearly £50-million for Cunard!

The charter continued until 4th June when the *QE2* sailed from Osaka to be later handed back to Cunard's charge in Honolulu, Hawaii. From here she made a five day cruise, starting 19th June, including calls at Lahaina and Kona, both in the Hawaiian Islands, and then a transpacific to Ensenada on the north-west coast of Mexico.

Transferring to San Diego a 13-day trip brought her from the US Westcoast through the Panama Canal, finally arriving in New York on 7th July, Independence Day having been spent at sea between St. Thomas and Ft. Lauderdale. A transatlantic return to Southampton brought her back to New York on 17th July in readiness for one of the most prestigious cruises of her career to date.

Whilst the ship had been on charter in Japan, it was announced in January that her home port of Southampton would be bestowing the Freedom of the City on both the *Queen Elizabeth 2* and her crew in the months to come. On making the announcement the Leader of the City Council described the *Queen Elizabeth 2* as "...a vessel that is very much alive and promoting the present and future of our city...across the world."

On 17th July *QE2* departed New York on the outset of a trip that would celebrate 150 years of the Cunard Line. Samuel Cunard's paddle steamer *Britannia* had been the first of his steamers to cross the Atlantic in 1840 leaving Liverpool on 4th July, arriving in Halifax, Nova Scotia, twelve-and-a-half days later, and finally reaching Boston where she was accorded a very warm welcome after a total passage from England of 14 days 8 hours.

It was essential that the *Queen* should arrive in the United Kingdom on time and to ensure that this was done the *QE2*, under the command of Captain Robin Woodall, achieved her fastest ever eastbound crossing of the Atlantic at an average speed of 30.16 knots and she arrived in British waters in 4 days, 6 hours and 57 minutes.

Shortly after the liner's arrival in the Hampshire port on 22nd July her Captain, on behalf of his ship and her crew, was ceremoniously presented with the Freedom of the City of Southampton, the towns highest honour, by the city's Mayor and Port Admiral, Councillor Mary Key. Never before had the honour been bestowed on so many people at the same time. Captain Woodall recalled that the Freedom meant that he could drive his sheep through the city's ancient Bargate!

From Southampton on 23rd July the *Queen Elizabeth 2* sailed on a 6-day, celebratory cruise that would take her in triumph around the British Isles.

Captain Robin Woodall receives the Freedom of the City of Southampton on behalf of the ship and her crew from the City's Mayor and Port Admiral, Mrs. Mary Key.
Southern Newspapers

Chapter Fifteen

A Cruise of Celebration

During the *Queen Elizabeth 2*'s very special "Cunard - 150 Years" cruise it seemed that all the country wanted to catch a glimpse of the worlds most famous liner as her reception in all of her ports of call was beyond the wildest dreams of those on board for this extra-gala occasion.

The liner would make a different port on each day of the cruise, beginning with Cobh (Cove) on Monday, 23rd July, 1990. Her arrival in the Irish port was scheduled for 7.30am and, as the liner came in past Roches Point and into the beautiful Cork Harbour, she was given a wonderful reception and was soon surrounded by dozens of yachts and other craft. Thousands upon thousands of people could be seen on the surrounding hills and headlands and great numbers of people could be seen around the city and St. Colemans Cathedral as the *Queen* approached her dock. Captain Woodall thought that the berthing position was a very narrow and small space in which to manoeuvre such a big ship but the weather was being kind with a calm sea .

The Trafalgar House "Dauphin 2" helicopter, piloted by Captain David Warren, had been embarked on the liner to fly dignitaries and press on and off the liner, and the ship's Captain was very proud of the fact that his vessel had been turned into "...a great, big aircraft carrier..." for the occasion of the cruise.

The Irish Republican Premier, Mr Charles Haughey, came on board and the *Queen Elizabeth 2* was guided into a new cargo terminal, at Ringaskiddy, which was being inaugurated by the *QE2*'s arrival. Units of the Irish Navy escorted the liner to her berth, the navy's commodore being on board the Cunarder.

The *QE2* sailed that evening at 7pm to the accompaniment of exploding fireworks and with the sky colourfully speckled with hundreds of balloons. Because of the later hour, there were also more people about to witness her departure, the surrounding hills blackened with the assembled crowds.

During the trip across the Atlantic there had been many special entertainments on board including the wonderful orchestra of The Academy of St. Martins-in-the-Fields. Peter Duchin and His Orchestra had played for the 150th Anniversary Ball and for the Round Britain Cruise Lester Lanin and His Orchestra played for the Royal and Grand Masked Balls and other special dances. The famed Royal Philharmonic Orchestra, under the baton of Andre Previn, would join the ship in Scotland.

The gala cruise progressed in triumph to perhaps the most important destination of the voyage - the Port of Liverpool from where the Cunard Lines story had originally begun in 1840.

Captain Robin Woodall had a special affection for this seaport as he lived on the Wirral, the prominatory opposite the Cheshire city.

The *Queen Elizabeth 2* was expected to be in the River Mersey in the morning of Tuesday, 24th July so the day had to start early for those on board. As the ship approached Anglesey at around six o'clock she steamed in close to pass near to the South Stack and, as the Holyhead lifeboat and a mass of small-craft came out to greet the liner, those on the ship who were already up and about could already see a lot of people on the shore and cliffs looking seawards towards them.

The *QE2* then steamed (even after her conversion to a motorship it is still hard to not use references to steam!) towards the Bar Light marking the mouth of the Mersey where she waited for sufficient water to enable her to safely pass over the sandbar that guards the entrance to Liverpools great river.

Once enough water was beneath her she started to move up the river. It was a beautiful, sunny day with a brisk South-east breeze and the *Queen* progressed in state on the flood tide towards the maritime city where an anticipated half-million people were expected to greet the liner.

Captain Woodall recalled the emotion of the moment: "I remember that the first inkling that I got of the massive crowds that would be there was looking at the shore at Crosby. I thought, well - that's funny! It looks black and it should be nice golden sands over at Crosby. And then I saw the sun glinting off literally hundreds of cars ...looking at it through the binoculars I could see that it was literally black with people! Amazing! And then.....as we closed into the river...looking at New Brighton (it, too, was) absolutely solid with people". Millions of people had been anticipated to see the ship arrive and it appeared that this estimate had been achieved!

The "embarked air", the Trafalgar House helicopter, was again busy bringing the mayors of Liverpool, The Wirral and Birkenhead out to the liner whilst members of the press joined the civic dignitaries on the Bridge to view the unfolding spectacle before them as the great ship progressed up the Mersey.

QE2 is berthed at Cobh during her triumphant call into the Irish Port as part of Cunard's 150th Anniversary celebratory cruise around the British Isles in 1990.   *Richard Weiss*

Chapter Sixteen

An Anniversary Fit For a Queen

The cold, overcast morning of Friday 27th July, 1990, was sullen with a threat of rain in the air. The Solent was in one of its unseasonable grey moods but this mood was fortunately not reflected by the atmosphere that prevailed on the water.

From Cherbourg *Queen Elizabeth 2* arrived at her position at the end of Voyage 749 at around 8.45am and anchored in her alloted position. Fifteen minutes later the containership *Atlantic Conveyor*, 58,438 tons and built in 1985 to replace her namesake that had been sunk during the 1982 Falklands conflict, took up her designated place (originally alloted to the *Vistafjord*) to the south-east of her fleet-mate and, after another similar period, the graceful, five-star *Vistafjord* (bought by the Cunard in 1983 from Norwegian Cruise Lines - although British built - she still retained her original grey hull) anchored, for some reason late, astern of the "box boat". The presence of these three ships represented perhaps the most famous shipping line in the world - the Cunard and the impending presence of Royal guests indicated the esteem in which the Line was held. An icon of the British Mercantile Marine, if not a national treasure.

Seven small vessels had also arrived at their Review positions and moored in line ahead, parallel to and to the north-west of the three huge ships. Amongst this secondary line were sailing craft (including the three year old sail training vessel constructed for the disabled, *Lord Nelson*, which included a mast donated by contributions from passengers and crew of the *QE2*) and auxiliary naval ships. By 9.15am the assemblage was complete.

Meanwhile, all around the area of the anchorage, dozens of private yachts and motor boats, as well as excursion vessels from nearby Portsmouth Harbour and Southampton, jostled for the best positions from which to witness the unfolding spectacle that surrounded them.

Having left Portsmouth Harbour at 9.25am the Royal Squadron soon appeared as the Royal Yacht *Britannia*, with Her Majesty Queen Elizabeth II and His Royal Highness The Duke of Edinburgh on board, came up astern to the port side of *Queen Elizabeth 2*. The Monarch aboard the Royal Yacht was preceded, as of tradition, by a Trinity House Vessel, the *Patricia*, and followed by Her Majesty's Ship *Broadsword*. Cheering passed over the waters from those on board the fleet to be reviewed.

The squadron passed the anchored ships before turning 180 degrees to progress past the portsides of the anchored Cunarders. The passengers on board the two liners lining the Boatdecks of their ships were again encouraged to give "Three cheers for Her Majesty, The Queen", Her Majesty, dressed in light blue, and her husband, HRH The Duke of Edinburgh, being clearly seen on the after deck of the graceful and, as always, impeccable *Britannia*.

The squadron then turned around the stern of the *Vistafjord* and sailed between the main and secondary lines of moored vessels. Meanwhile, the first of two aerial tributes flew overhead as the elegant airliner "Concorde" made an appearance followed by a Britannia Airways Boeing 767, a heavy-lift "Belfast" and a Boeing 747 of Virgin Airways.

As the Royal Yacht anchored ahead of the reviewed fleet at 11.20am a second fly pass ocurred, comprising of "Sea King", "Lynx" and "Dauphin" helicopters and a "Sea Harrier" jump-jet.

The Royal Barge was lowered from its parent vessel and, accompanied by police and naval launches, was soon churning the choppy waters of The Solent towards the lowered, portside accommodation ladder of the *Queen Elizabeth 2*, approaching the liner from around her stern.

The Royal party embarked *Queen Elizabeth 2* at noon, being greeted on the ship by Captain Woodall (who had made a dash down from the Bridge), Sir Nigel Broackes, Eric Parker and Bernard Crisp, Cunard's UK director. Introductions were then made to the Chief Engineer, Steve Hare; Staff Chief Engineer John Tomlins; Hotel Manager John Duffy and Staff Captain Ron Bolton. As the Sovereign was now on board, her Standard was broken-out from the masthead.

A reception followed in the Queen's Room where Her Majesty met Captain and Mrs Alan Bennell. Captain Bennell was still officially Master of *Queen Elizabeth 2* but had been suffering from poor health and had been ashore on sick-leave for some time.

As the Queen came down the stairway to the Grand Lounge she was greeted by a fanfare

During the Anniversary Review HM The Queen and HRH The Duke of Edinburgh responded to cheers and applause from those on board the assembled ships.
Richard Weiss

The Royal party was then escorted to the Bridge where the Queen and the Duke of Edinburgh were introduced to Relief Captain Ron Warwick who was conning the ship and both royal personages showed great interest in the activity around them.

3.40pm - and the *Queen Elizabeth 2* berthed at the Queen Elizabeth II Terminal at Southampton's Dock Head. Captain Woodall escorted his royal guests to the gangway before handing them into the care of the Lord Lieutenant of Hampshire.

A most significant and memorable day, indeed week, in the career of the *Queen Elizabeth 2* drew to a successful close (complete with a Cunard marquee on the Town Quay and more fireworks) as she lay at her berth in the River Test with the *Vistafjord* astern of her as a companion. The larger ship would sail the next day, Saturday 28th July, for New York on a transatlantic crossing, her third of four celebratory 150th Anniversary Cruises.

Above: On boarding the liner Her Majesty Queen Elizabeth II unveiled a plaque to commemorate the event. The Queen would then travel the 20 miles to Southampton on board the ship, the first ever such trip that she had made since she had launched the vessel in 1967. *Cunard*

Right: A good study showing the great width of *Queen Elizabeth 2,* alongside at Cobh, Ireland on 23rd July 1990. Later, in 1994, there would be various modifications to her stern arrangements. *Richard Weiss*

played by The Royal Philharmonic Orchestra. Her Majesty then unveiled a plaque to commemorate her visit to the ship on this important anniversary.

During the luncheon that followed the other vessels that had taken part in the review had dispersed leaving the *QE2* the last to leave the anchorage, doing so at 1.45pm. Again led by the *THV Patricia* the Cunarder made her way through The Solent and up Southampton Water towards Southampton. Remarkably, this would be the first time that Her Majesty The Queen had sailed in the liner that she had launched 27 years earlier.

After lunch Captain Woodall escorted the Queen through the various public rooms of his ship and Her Majesty seemed to enjoy the whole ocassion. Passengers, corralled by red-rope restraints, lined the royal route through the vessel, having previously being given coloured coded tickets by Cruise Director Peter Longley's staff which indicated in which part of the liner they should wait.

endeavours of many people in both artistic and technical fields came to a climax on 13th November when *Queen Elizabeth 2* arrived in New York and, after disembarking her passengers, was taken out of service and sailed directly to Blohm + Voss shipyard in on the River Elbe in Hamburg, Germany. Her scheduled sailing to Southampton did not materialise.

Here she was to have a radical refit involving her interiors (furnishings and layouts), structural alterations, and a new overall look. It would, as the publicists' had said earlier in the year when initial designs had been published, enable the ship to "....sail into the Twenty First Century....". It was also said that, as the *QE2* had been "....twenty-five years ahead of her time...", she had really caught up with herself and that it was time to enable her to compete in the market place not in direct competition with much younger, glitzier cruise ships but as a by-now classic liner in her own right.

For many weeks prior to the ship's withdrawal from paying passenger service contractors had systematically sealed off blocks of cabins and, after the cabins had been checked for "fibre", started to prepare the rooms for the forthcoming refurbishment and structural alterations. All 963 cabins were intended to have new bathrooms, a huge logistical undertaking in itself - and one that would lead to problems in the future weeks - and work was also planned to be undertaken on minor stairwells during these preceding voyages. From July, up to 120 skilled men completed preparations in sixty units in each ten-day period, and over three hundred items (many from other suppliers who in turn had to be sub-contracted) required for each cabin's update were stored in a dockside shed in Southampton in readiness for transference to the ship during her short turn-arounds.

At around this time the ship's doctor, Nigel Roberts, author in 1988 of "C-Six: Ten Years as the Doctor of the *QE2*" (C-Six being not only a pun for *mal-de-mer* but also the location of the ship's well-equipped hospital) was made "redundant". This was, he believed, a result of protesting against the lack of protection given to crew members during the removal of residue asbestos from the ship.

The refurbishment was planned to complete so that the *Queen Elizabeth 2* could undertake a two-day shake-down cruise before leaving Southampton on her scheduled 17th December sailing for New York prior to the start of her 1995 world cruise. £30-million was the expected cost of the whole work. The four weeks alloted was a very short time indeed for such a major job and left no room, it seemed, for delay. Accountancy appeared to have the upper hand once again over ship husbandry.

Two teams of specialist designers had been employed by Cunard to undertake the interior re-styling of their world-famous ship - MET Studio Ltd., and John McNeece Ltd., - both companies, a statement said, "...working together to create a unified design concept which will re-establish the rhythm and harmony of the ship's spaces in keeping with the spirit of this unique, ocean-going liner".

Both companies would also, continued the statement, "...work on aspects of the interior design, with MET Studio (MET was headed by Alex McCuaig who had begun his career with James Gardner, the original masterplanner for the ship) responsible for the masterplanning and interior design and (John) McNeece responsible for project management and (also) interior design". A unity of interior design and an easy flow of passengers were the keys to the new-look *QE2*.

Structurally the changes to the *Queen's* internal layout

Always an impressive image, a mighty ocean liner high and dry in a floating dock.   *Cunard*

would reflect the foresight of her designers in arranging her public rooms (except for the theatre and the Grand Lounge, ex-Double Down Room) on one deck level which gave greater flexibility should the need arise to reconfigure these spaces. That time had arrived.

Included amongst the many changes planned were:

Sun Deck- a small bar and toilets aft of the superstructure block were built for the convenience of the sun worshippers using this delightful sheltered deck.

Boat Deck- additional shops were built around the well of the Grand Lounge, the "International Shopping Concourse" being renamed the "Royal Promenade" and the floors were given inlays of woods in compass form; the Conference Room was renamed the Boardroom; theatre balcony refurbished; and the Queen's Grill and Lounge were also refurbished.

Upper Deck- the Yacht Club Bar was destined to become even more popular with its refit. Expanding forward the Club extended to spaces previously occupied by the Tour Office, the Teen Club; whilst various toilets and stairways were dispensed with. A foyer to the Club was also built and would boast some of the Cunard Heritage Trail artefacts including a portrait of Samuel Cunard and the sumptuous silver loving cup (presented to him with other silver by the grateful citizens of Boston after the first arrival there of the paddler *Britannia*) that had been previously displayed in the Colombia Restaurant on Quarter Deck. The Players Casino, portside amidships was given a small bar and paintings of interiors of the *Queen Mary*; the Theatre Bar, starboard, was changed into a British pub, called the "Golden Lion" in honour of the rampant creature on the company's flag; and the after end of the Mauretania Restaurant disappeared to create a transverse meeting area, the Crystal Bar with *Art Deco* motifs, including a reproduction of a flying horse based on a relief previously used on the old *Queen Elizabeth*. A small, attractive stairwell was installed on the port side, to match that on the starboard side that served the Princess Grill Starboard (now renamed the Britannia Grill) to give access to the Princess Grill. The remainder of the Mauretania Restaurant underwent a remarkable transformation and was restyled to become the 580-seat Caronia Restaurant, decorated in a colour scheme to reflect the colours of the "Green Goddess". The partitions along each side were given large, glazed curves and a large aluminium sculpture by Althea Wynne was placed in the middle of the room. This depicted several horses in wave-like action and reflected the horse motifs used extensively on the *Caronia*, of 1949. A mural of the "Goddess" by Jane Human adorned the rooms forward bulkhead whilst the builders model of the *Caronia* along with her original builders plate and a superb painting of that ship at Cape Town by master marine artist Stephen Card greeted diners as they made their entrance.

Quarter Deck- the Magrodome that had been fitted over the Lido area in 1983 to make the swimming pool usable even on the Atlantic run was removed. This retractable cover had had a mixed reception; one of the main criticisms was that, after rain, the cover showered passengers with water when it was retracted! The Lido Cafe was decked over, the decking above providing additional sunning area; the pool was removed; and stairways were constructed to One Deck below to a new, airy, enclosed Pavilion self-service hamburger grill and bar overlooking the One Deck swimming pool. The Cafe would be used for informal dining and the famous Midnight Buffets! Self-service buffet bars port and starboard were replaced by a new Tour and Travel Office; a Social Director's Office; and new toilets. The twin stairways forward of the Grand Lounge were removed to

Above: The magnificent silver Loving Cup that was bestowed on Captain Woodruff of the Cunard paddle steamer *Britannia* by the grateful citizens of Boston, Massachusetts, in 1840. The cup's location outside the Yacht Club bar makes a splendid spot from which to start the on-board Heritage Trail that was installed during the 1994 refit.   *Author*

Below: Decorating a panel in the Crystal Bar outside the 1994 Caronia Restaurant is this bas relief that reflects those installed on the *Queen Elizabeth* of 1939.   *Author*

make way for a larger stage and a new, sprung dance floor was sited further aft towards the stage; a smaller stairway placed aft was in a similar position to the original spiral stairway of 1969 and the Lounge was refurbished to give better views of the stage. The tan-brown leather cubist armchairs were disposed of (one always had a propensity to slide out of them!) and replaced with smaller chairs in a light mustard yellow. Carpeting was also changed. Wood veneers lined the Lounge, reflecting a return to this traditional material in other areas of the ship. Forward again and, starboard, the Midships Bar (always dark and cosy with its green suede walls) was opened up and brightened with a new bar, more artefacts (including Captain Peter Jackson's sextant on a five-year loan); and a grand piano, hailing from the *Queen Mary*, transferred from the Midships Lobby. Port, the popular Library was extended forward using the Card Room to become the Book Shop, doubling the Library's overall capacity. A corridor leading to a stairway divided the two rooms. A vaulted, glazed ceiling gave one the feel of a social hall on a nineteenth century steamer. The *QE2's* Librarian remained the only full-time librarian at sea and a second would be employed. Columbia Restaurant became the 464-seat Mauretania, the latter having been transferred from the deck above. The large painting of the four-funnelled *Mauretania* was hung here having been transferred from a corner of the Quarter Deck outside the old Card Room entrance where it had been hopelessly out of scale with its surroundings. Princess and Britannia Grills completed the public rooms on this deck.

One Deck- the Beauty Salon was enlarged; and the Princess Grill (Port) Lounge was dispensed with as the attractive Crystal Bar on Upper Deck would suffice both Grills for pre-dinner cocktails.

Other than alterations to the *QE2* Spa and Gymnasium the other major alteration involved the spectacular, circular Midships Lobby which has always served both as the main entrance to the ship and as a room for small or recorded concerts whilst at sea. Built with a space-age ceiling and decorated in dark green and black it would be altered with wood burr veneered, quadrant balustrades enclosing the central recessed well. Long murals painted by Peter Sutton depicting events in the history of the Cunard Line in a montage style were displayed on the surrounding walls, giving embarking passengers an instant appreciation of the traditions that lay behind the company's history, including a picture of the "Q4" on the slip as shown earlier in this book. It had been intended to raise the ceiling of the Lobby through two decks with a balcony around the One Deck level but this (perhaps fortunately) did not happen. The *QE2* Computer Learning centre on this deck was also reduced in length.

Although it was regretted that, by now, the United Kingdom had lost the shipyards with the necessary skills to perform such work more than half of the workforce of skilled men came to Germany from Britain under contract. Blohm + Voss were ideally placed to undertake the work as they had worked on the *Queen* several times before. But Ron Connolly, Cunard's senior Technical Director, and others had misgivings about completing such a heavy workload in the short time available. Work continued around the clock and in crowded conditions on the ship as she lay in Floating Dock 11 in an attempt to meet the very tight deadline.

As with much construction and complex plumbing work (and ships notoriously present unexpected problems in such areas) the timetable for the refit fell enough behind schedule to delay the finishing trades (upholsterers, soft furnishings, etc) from starting their work and by the time that the *Queen Elizabeth 2* arrived in Southampton the work was far from complete. A lady writing to the London "Times" said "Sir, Renovations on our bathroom started in 1993, three weeks before Christmas.... I had my first shower in July 1994 and the floor has yet to be laid. I offer Cunard...... my heartfelt sympathies." Understanding came from other informed quarters (including journalist Alan Coren, the son of a plumber and himself a one-time plumbers mate, also writing in "The Times") but the Cunard management was criticised for demanding such heavy expectations from project managers in the various sub-contracting firms.

Plumbing work in some cabins was still being worked on; carpets in some areas lay still rolled; boxes - full and empty - were piled all over the ship; rubbish skips adorned the after decks ready for being craned off. Workmen and women were busy everywhere - sitting on floors sewing curtains, attempting to finish the Grand Lounge with scaffolding platforms filling the dancefloor; chairs and cardboard boxes crowding the Queen's Room.

Captain Ron Warwick toured his ship wearing a look of resigned disbelief. Meanwhile passengers were eagerly congregating in the Queen Elizabeth II Terminal ashore waiting to board the ship, not yet knowing that the seeming chaos that prevailed on board was worse than anticipated. Workmen could be seen through the ship's windows working on bunches of trailing cables that hung in bunches from open ceiling panels.

Originally a two-day celebration cruise to the English Channel had been scheduled on the ship's return to the UK on 14th December but this jaunt was yet another victim of the existing unhappy state of affairs.

Between 15th and 17th December stability tests were carried out, the ship being inclined with heavy weights moved from one side of the vessel to the other in order to establish her metacentric height.

Meanwhile, formalities still had to be observed and HRH Prince Andrew, The Duke of York, arrived at Southampton on sailing day, 17th December, to unveil two royal portraits temporarily sited in the Queen's Room for the occasion. The larger of these portraits was of HM Queen Elizabeth the Queen Mother (painted when she was still Queen), painted by Sir Oswald Birley, and had hung in the Main Lounge of the *Queen Elizabeth*. After that great ship's sale to American interests, the picture was given on permanent loan to Southampton City Council and hung in the Mayor's parlour.

The other painting, by Edward Halliday, portrayed Queen Elizabeth II when, as Princess Elizabeth, she had married Lieutenant Philip Mountbatten RN. The painting, mounted in a contemporary, specially carved frame, showed them arm-in-arm as the Duke and Duchess of Edinburgh and had been originally hung in the Main Lounge of the legendary *Caronia*. This latter oil-painting had also been handed into the care of Southampton's council on that ships decommissioning from Cunard and was eventually placed above the magnificent stairway inside the entrance hall of the town's post-war Civic Centre.

Twenty five years previously Cunard's deputy chairman, Lord Mancroft, had handed the paintings over to Southampton "...for all time". Now a Cunard spokesman said "They are Cunard's paintings and while we are happy for them to be in Southampton we feel that the *QE2* is the embodiment of Southampton". With that an intimation was dropped that the pictures would be returned to the city should the *QE2* be de-commissioned.

It nevertheless came as a blow to Southamptons civic pride when Cunard asked for the return of the paintings for the *Queen Elizabeth 2*. They were subsequently hung either side of the forward main stairwell landing between Upper and Quarter Decks.

As the Duke of York pulled the cord to unveil the paintings the curtains stuck. A royal tug only managed to dislodge the rail holding the curtains, one side of which collapsed like a dipped flag over the side of the exposed painting of The Queen Mother! Captain Burton-Hall undoubtedly did his best to make light of the situation. The shambles of the occasion only seemed to reflect the seeming chaos that the unfinished state of the liners interior presented to the press.

The Duke, who had previously toured the ship and had seen the unfinished state of a vessel in refit - a condition that he sympathised with from his own experiences in the Royal Navy - was quietly taken off the ship in order to avoid protests from the increasingly impatient passengers waiting to board the liner for their Christmas cruise to New York.

Chapter Twenty One

Transmutation to Magnificence

Three hundred people from just over one thousand booked for the crossing had had their transatlantic Christmas voyage tickets cancelled before they had left home but several hundred more had arrived at the Terminal expecting their cabins to be ready. But disappointments were again in store as one hundred and sixty more were informed that they could not sail with the ship. The workload still remaining and the state of many cabins had convinced the local Inspector from the Marine Safety Office that the ship should only sail with a thousand passengers - and this number would have to include the army of skilled workmen who would, of necessity, travel with the ship to complete their work. He issued a certificate to that effect. Refunds and promises of a free cruise were offered, but some of the erstwhile passengers baulked at the idea of the free cruise. Six hundred fare-paying passengers would board the liner. The liner's post-refit capacity should have been around 1,760.

Eighty passengers boarding the ship knew that when the ship sailed they still would not have been allocated cabins. Frequent floods had occurred and some cabins were deep in water. Two maritime authors who had been visiting the ship disembarked and, as they did so, were met by two reporters from the local BBC television station, one of whom was obviously upset - as were many other members of the press - at having her ticket cancelled. On being asked about the condition of the ship one of the authors responded "She's in a state typical of a ship under refit. But when she is finished she will be magnificent!"

And magnificent she would be. Through the current state of the liner's interior the prospect of a new, integrated decor could be seen that would live up to the company's expectations. Gone were the remnants of piecemeal refits and an unified interior gave the impression of a ship that would again achieve her old popularity as soon as the embarrassments, disappointments, inconveniences and "anti-Cunard" press had been forgotten.

The use of wood veneers (beech, American cherry, mahogany, etc,), and of carefully chosen colours in the carpeting was the first impression of the new layout. Then the awareness of the history of the Cunard unfolded as displays and models were discovered on the new Heritage Trail. A huge model of the old "Maury" stood outside the new Mauretania Restaurant, its case supports not yet enclosed with panelling; a statue, "The Spirit of the Sea", that used to grace the First Class Lounge of the second Mauretania, was displayed near the Midships Lobby, itself in stark contrast to its predecessor; the new Caronia Restaurant with its models, paintings,

After such a major overhaul the QE2 was famously not ready for her 1994 Christmas Cruise to New York much to the disappointment - and annoyance - of many. However, the promise of a magnificent new look shone through the apparent disarray.
Southern Newspapers

sweeping glass partitions, a huge, illuminated sculpture of horses with a fountain at its base, a mural on the aft bulkhead showing the "Green Goddess" in an exotic location; the Crystal Bar; the new Midships Bar perhaps not quite so intimate now as it had been although it now boasted the piano from the *Queen Mary* that had been transfereed from the Midships Lobby and a case of navigational memorabilia including ex-Captain Peter Jackson's sextant displayed on loan for five years.

Artworks were also added, but the gallery created on the bulkheads of a corridor proved to be unpopular as it made the location look like a small shop without adequate viewing space. Paintings by artists Stephen Card, Harley Crossley and Simon Fisher graced the after stairwell where their paintings positioning and space gave them a greater impact.

In the attractive, rebuilt and extended Library and Bookshop the staff bravely worked like Trojans within the unfinished rooms, polishing and tidying as well as stocking the shelves. Six hundred additional volumes were added to the six thousand already on the shelves. A second Librarian was employed as a result of the expansion.

Ease of passenger movement and access had been a prime remit in the designers' brief and passenger flow around the ship, including ramps and toilets for the disabled, was vastly improved as a result. Lighting, too, was an important element, which was used to great effect with the *Art Deco* inspired interiors.

Externally the *Queen Elizabeth 2* looked magnificent in her new colour scheme, although her brilliant white superstructure had been given what could only be described as a "Go Faster Stripe" in red, gold and royal blue. Self-adhesive and two hundred metres long it was placed along a level between One and Quarter Decks extending fore and aft

from below the Bridge to the Lido Cafe. At the forward end of the stripe was the Cunard lion, painted in gold outline with the existing legend "CUNARD" emblazoned in red above; over the line at the after end, was the beflagged Trafalgar House logo. The stripe itself was in Trafalgar House colours and was of the type that could be seen stuck onto hoardings surrounding the company's building sites. Appropriate, perhaps, because at this particular moment in time the *QE2* herself resembled a building site!

Quite stunningly, the hull of *Queen Elizabeth 2* had been painted in royal blue. The boot-topping remained the standard red anti-fouling but, between boot-topping and dark blue hull a waterline was painted of a surprising yellow/gold. As this thin line was usually painted a smart white the new colour gave a feeling of oily, faded neglect. In spite of that, the *Queen* looked the superliner that she was.

With workmen still on board, the ship sailed several hours late leaving many disgruntled passengers ashore. As the embarked workmen had to be accommodated somewhere they were given cabins on Five Deck (which, of course, decreased further the number of fare-paying passengers that could be carried), sharing facilities as work was proceeding around the clock.

Passengers were inconvenienced during the crossing by floods (ship's staff being notified of such events over the broadcast system by the call "Niagara! Niagara!"), dripping water, uncarpeted floors, piles of bedding in the theatre (which were soon cleared), toilets and washing facilities that ran with rusty brown water, erupting toilets, etc, etc,. One of the few finished spaces was the Britannia Grill which was described as "...an oasis", offering a haven of peace from the uproar around the ship. A Force 8 during the trip also took its toll on some of the workmen who, suffering from sea-sickness, delayed their work even more.

Both crew (many of whom were upset at what had befallen their ship), supernumery staff such as superintendants and officers, and the Safety Inspector kept a vigilant watch to ensure that satisfactory levels of safety were maintained and advising appropriate action where doors and corridors were found to be temporarily obstructed by equipment, waste materials, etc. Barges had been ordered ahead of arrival in New York to ship away the accumulated garbage which was stored aft on One Deck, a convenient location in readiness for off-loading.

The ship arrived in New York twelve hours late because of the bad weather experienced and, to save time, United States Coast Guard personnel boarded the ship earlier than expected to inspect the ship prior to issuing their certificate of "Control Verification for a Foreign Vessel". Cunard's chairman John Olsen, appointed by Trafalgar Houses main shareholder - Hong Kong Land - also boarded to negotiate with angry and disappointed passengers.

One of the passengers to sail on the *QE2* in 1997 was 85 year old Millvina Dean. At just a few weeks old she had been the youngest survivor of the foundering of the *Titanic* in 1912. The *Queen Elizabeth 2* is seen here (with Millvina on board) passing the ancient castle at Calshot at the entrance to Southampton Water. It would be Millvina's first ocean voyage since returning from America all those years ago.   *Author*

Queen Elizabeth 2 moored at her usual berth in Southampton during 1995. She is sporting her new deep blue hull with the Trafalgar House 'go-faster' stripe on the superstructure.

Roger Hardingham

The conditions that the USCG found gave rise to concern. The expected barges were now unavailable so the rubbish had to be manhandled down through the ship to a shell door in the ship's side and this task started a few hours before the ship arrived in New York. The USCG's impression was that the rubbish had been piled inside the ship all through the voyage.

Without meeting any senior staff to discuss the reasons and solutions for the problems that the Coastguards found and to put the problems into context, the USCG wandered unaccompanied and freely about the vessel speaking to members of the crew, therefore not receiving an authoritative overall picture of the prevailing conditions. By the time that senior staff were eventually consulted the USCG had "...already become convinced that the ship was in a dangerous condition".

Even so, the required Certificate was issued after it was ascertained that certain work would be undertaken, such as disposal of the garbage (a major job which was already underway) and that fire-doors that had been wedged open for ease of working (but had been kept monitored during the voyage) were safe. The certificate restricted access to certain areas of the ship. The MSA had issued the ship with a full term Passenger Certificate in Britain on the understanding that the garbage would be cleared before sailing from New York on the World Cruise and that certain other works (mainly revolving around the new Lido) would be completed as soon as possible during that trip.

The USCG inspectors presented the company with six pages of requests to remedy safety violations some of which, without their knowledge, had been previously verbally highlighted by the MSA. The certificate for a reduced number of passengers that had been issued in Southampton was intended to keep passengers out of the rebuilt Lido area but the USCG was not aware of this restriction and declared that passengers should be resticted completely from using the vertical "Fire Zone 7" which included not only the Lido but the decks above and below it as well. The MSA inspector also thought that the USCG had the impression "....that most of the work carried out in New York would not have been done had they not specifically asked for it" although it had been already planned or was even underway.

The press had a field-day and it was not only Cunard and the *Queen Elizabeth 2* that received their attention. Personalities within Cunard unfortunately got drawn into the mud-slinging; the MSA inspector, too, was slated for having his wife accompany him (the reports omitted to mention that she also worked for the MSA - one punny headline read "*QE2* Waives the Rules") and for several weeks the mere mention of the ship's name brought forth negative comments from a generally unempathetic press. At least, many of the newspaper cartoons expressed an amusement over the reports in the media.

Another difficulty arose before the ship was able to leave New York. Because of the USCG report - and also unbeknown to Cunard - the ship had been prohibited from sailing until all the defects in the report had been rectified. A Detention Notice was usually issued to the ship but, in this case, it was not. Instead an unlogged telephone call had been made to the British Consulate in New York and its recipient at the Consulate later remembered receiving the call but not the message that a Notice had been issued. It was only when a letter was received from Admiral Card of the USCG that the seriousness of the situation became apparent and a series of meetings were hurriedly held in Washington and New York in order to resolve the *impasse*.

The ship was eventually permitted to sail - twenty four hours late (the work remaining being completed over the following few days) on her World Cruise leaving behind recriminations, claims and counter-claims. A lawyer who had experienced the Christmas cruise and representing several other passengers went to Cunard's London office to picket the company and to lodge his complaints. The early television news showed him rattling an office door and claiming that Cunard had locked him out (good television!) Unfortunately, he was rattling the secure, corner door that was only used by staff: he was shown on a later news bulletin entering Cunard's offices through the large revolving doors at 30-35 Pall Mall! He later expressed his satisfaction with his compensation.

Hard lessons had been learned and improvements in communications, surveys and line management would result. The final "victim" of the whole unhappy episode was John Olsen, Cunard's chairman since 1993. He had approved the refit and had been the man with the courage to exploit Cunard's history in such a grand way on the ship. He admitted in January that the *QE2* should not have sailed before the refit had been completed and was dismissed from the company the following May with a compensation for "...loss of office..." of £232,000. Olsen was replaced by Peter Ward, lately chairman of Rolls Royce, who was apparently not so keen on the Heritage aspects of the ship and rumours of the planned removal of the increasingly popular artefact cases abounded on the waterfront.

In one way the *Queen Elizabeth 2* had grown in stature during the refit. Her Gross Tonnage (1 Gross Ton = 100 cubic feet) had changed over the years since her design (58,000gt projected); entry into service (65,862); increasing after various refits to 67,139 in 1985; reducing slightly (66,450) in 1988: 69,053 (1991) and, in 1994, she was entered in Lloyd's Register as being of 70,327 gross tons. Some things had remained as they were: her call sign "GBTT" and her Official Number 336703.

Perhaps because of the adverse publicity that *QE2* had received from the post-refit press, she would achieve a new popularity in the months and years to come.

There seemed to be nothing more appealing to the travelling public in 1995 than a *Queen* with a tarnished reputation!!

Part of the refit work that continued at Southampton and during the Christmas Cruise.   *David Ellery*

Above: The Midship's Bar in 2000. Gone is the more inimate darker look but a brighter bar for cruising is now evident. *Peter Seden*
Below: Stylish vaulted ceilings in the Library give the room a feel of the old Cunarders. *Inset:* The same room as it appeared at the end of the 1994 retit immediately prior to the Chrismas cruise! *Cunard/David Ellery*

Above: The Lobby to the Caronia Restaurant still boasts the large model of the *Mauretainia*.
Below: The new-look port Caronia Restaurant in 2000. Wood encased columns contribute to a more traditional look.   *Both, Peter Seden*

Above: The Midship's Lobby, the first interior that greets boarding passengers as they came aboard, was completely redesigned in the 1994 refit.

Below: The restyled Queen's Room with its gold upholstery and a carpet of gold Tudor roses on a royal blue background. *Both, Peter Seden*

Above: QE2's boat deck with the sparkling evening lights of Liverpool's famous buildings during its visit in 1990.

Left: The Britannia Grill. The print on the wall depicts the paddle steamer *Britannia* leaving Boston after a channel had been cut out of the ice by its citizens thus helping her to maintain a mail contract with the city.   *Cunard*

Below: The massive interior of the Engine Room during the 1987 refit. This panoramic photographic illustrates the vastness of the area and the complexity of the work involved. The first of the new engines can be seen already in place. Removed inner bottom plates to the left expose the structure beneath.   *Meyer Werft*

Above: The liner at Capetown with the dramatic Table Mountain overshadowing the southern-most city of South Africa.
Below: Another of *QE2*'s ports of call on her World Cruise schedule is San Francisco.

Cunard
Marvin Jensen

Chapter Twenty Two

Storms Abating and Arising

After passing through the Caribbean where some on-board problems still persisted (resulting in around six hundred other passengers having their cruises cancelled), the outstanding work from the refit was completed and the furore was generally left behind her. It was now hoped that the *Queen Elizabeth 2* could complete her 1995 World Cruise free of adverse publicity. But the eyes of the world's press were still on her, waiting in the sidelines for her next transgression.

Even whilst the ship was away, newspapers were full of American legal proceedings against Cunard amounting to claims of $100,000 for each American passenger (120 of them) as compensation, £7.5-million was put aside by

Cunard as a contingency to cover compensation claims. A year later settlements were reached, paying the UK to New York passengers $5,000 each and the New York to the Caribbean passengers $2,000.

Viscount Gochen, British Governmental Minister for Shipping, was also kept busy in the House of Lords responding to questions tabled by various Members of Parliament. The Viscount's reply began: "A report on the *QE2* incident has been completed by the Director of Operations and Seafarer Standards of the Marine Safety Agency. The Director's report discloses serious deficiencies in the shore and ship management of the vessel by Cunard; it also identifies failings on the part of the Marine Safety Agency". Criticism of the MSA fell short of the inquiry that MPs had demanded but did recommend several improvements in the Agency's procedures.

Passing into the Pacific Ocean the "new look" *QE2* was delighting recently-joined passengers but she was sailing into yet more controversy when she arrived at anchorage in Hawaiis Kailua Bay. Whilst there she was accused of spilling sewage into the sea. Hawaiis Maritime Law Enforcement Division rightly investigated and it was found that the muddy, swilling discharge was permitted waste pumped from the ship's garbage macerators possibly mixed with rusty residue from the water tanks.

The early Spring brought with it the news that James Gardner, who had designed much of the *QE2's* interiors and co-ordinated the ship's external original aesthetic appearance, had died at the age of 87.

The 117-day 1995 World Cruise (fares from £12,495 to £117,230 for the full cruise) ended in Southampton on 13th April, 1995. The year was divided into her by-now usual transatlantics; cruises down the US East Coast or to the Caribbean; North Cape to see the midnight sun in July and, in late August, the *QE2* made her first complete circumnavigation of the British Isles, calling at Guernsey, Waterford, Liverpool, Greenock and then Invergordon and the Tyne *en-route* down through the North Sea to Le Havre before returning to Southampton. However, the call into the Tyne (where a shipyard had made a bid for the 'Q3' contract) was cancelled due to the

Left top: The large, impressive and inwardly illuminated model of the old *Mauretania* of 1906 that stands in the foyer to the 1994 installed Mauretania (now Caronia) Restaurant.

Left below: This portrait of the then Princess Elizabeth shows her as the Duchess of Edinburgh with her new husband, the Duke of Edinburgh, and originally hung in the *Caronia*, the 'Green Goddess'. The painting, still in its original specially carved frame, now graces a stairwell on the *Queen Elizabeth 2*. *Both by Peter Seden*

prevailing rough conditions. The Mayor of Newcastle-on-Tyne and other local dignitaries were most disappointed as the liner steamed by in the gloom and the eagerly awaited reception on board disappeared with the liner.

It was also in April that Captain Warwick had the bow crest of the Cunard Lion removed from the *Cunard Countess*, which had been sold, and had it remounted on *QE2's* Bridge front when he joined her in September.

The fiftieth anniversary of the Allied victory over Hitler's Nazism - Victory in Europe (VE Day) - was celebrated in a special "VE Day Commemoration" cruise which took *QE2* to Gibraltar, Lisbon and then on to anchor off Plymouth (8th May), thereby making her maiden call at the famous Devonshire port and home of Sir Francis Drake, sailed on to Guernsey in the Channel Islands and returning home to Southampton.

June saw another sad departure when Captain William Law died on the 4th. Captain Law had been in command of the *QE2* during the bomb hoax of 1972 and had been in command of all three "Queen" liners. Later that month, during a transatlantic, Captain John Burton-Hall gave permission to hold and then led a small, early morning private commemoration service held to remember those lost in the Atlantic and Russian convoys during the Second World War. A wreath was cast into the sea.

The North Cape was visited again in July and as part of this cruise *QE2* called at Edinburgh on 17th July. HRH The Princess Anne came aboard for lunch. When the ship sailed around 3pm, the next day she led the sailing ships partaking in the "Cutty Sark" Tall Ships Race out through the Firth of Forth.

In mid-season the *Queen Elizabeth 2* celebrated another remarkable achievement - her One Thousandth voyage. This was achieved appropriately during an eastbound voyage between New York (an aircraft here towed a banner reading "NY salutes *QE2* on her 1000th voyage") and Southampton, 14th to 19th June, with fireboats sending up plumes of water in salute on both sides of the Atlantic. Special certificates and enamelled lapel badges in the form of the liners funnel were issued to both passengers and crew and a celebratory dinner was held during the crossing. 3.8-million miles were "on the clock" and some 1.7-million passengers had been carried during *QE2's* remarkable career.

The *Queen's* 1001st voyage took her to the Baltic calling at Copenhagen, Stockholm and Oslo. She was sent off from Southampton in gala style and similar gifts and dinners were enjoyed during this special cruise. Veteran singing star Edmund Hockridge was booked to perform in the Grand Lounge. He had sung there on *QE2's* maiden voyage when this room was the then brand-new Double Down Room.

On 7th September the *Queen* had left Southampton under the command of Captain Ron Warwick on another of her "Transatlantic Classic" voyages to New York. The usual Great Circle route was followed and soon the progress of Hurricane "Luis" (coming up from the Caribbean) was being carefully monitored and plotted on the Bridge. It was soon realised by the navigators that "Luis" would pass close to the course of the *QE2* and, on 10th September, the ships course was changed to the south-west in an attempt to distance the ship from the storm. The Captain reckoned that "Luis" would pass ahead of the *Queen* at eleven o'clock that evening and had accordingly informed the passengers, updating the information during the course of the day.

By late evening (Sunday, 10th September), with the "eye" of "Luis" still 140-miles, away the wind speed

had increased from 50 to 100 knots, giving the ship a heel of 7° to starboard. The wind then came from ahead creating very heavy head seas that continually broke over the ship's bow leaving it awash for minutes at a time. The seas had made it unadvisable for the hotel staff to set out the Midnight Buffet.

Speed was reduced and in the early hours of the morning the *QE2* hove-to, riding 30 to 40-foot waves. At 2.10am a rogue wave was sighted.

In her cabin Librarian June Applebee, prepared by the Captain's bulletins, prepared for the worst: "...I took the usual seaman-like precautions and put away any loose objects, even putting the telephone in the drawer, and settled down for a bumpy night.

"At about 2am I awoke with a start to find that both my wardrobe doors and the bathroom door had burst open! Never had that happened before".

"I turned on the television to Channel 3 - the TV camera above the Bridge (that gave a continuous view over the bow) - and turned off all the lights in the cabin. Being night time the screen was dark...gradually my eyes became accustomed to the darkness and I was able to make out a very dim definition of the bow of the ship".

"It was possible to see the waves breaking over the bow - which, in a storm, I have often seen in daylight - this was a very grey shadow around the darker bow...suddenly the screen appeared to be filling up with grey shadows - the ship was bumping around and I thought this was not normal - so I tried to put a pillow over my head and tried to get to sleep".

"The next morning we were told of the ...wave!"

On the Bridge Captain Warwick had kept a vigilant watch with his navigators and watchkeepers. He recalled the heart-stopping moment as hundreds of tons of water thundered down onto the foredeck of his ship: "The wave seemed to take ages to reach us, but it was probably less than a minute before it broke with tremendous force over the bow of the *QE2*. An incredible shudder went through the ship followed a few moments later by two smaller shudders. At the same time the sea was cascading all over the fore part of the ship, including the Bridge, and it was several seconds before the water had drained away from the wheelhouse windows and vision ahead was restored".

Cruise Director Brian Price was in his cabin on 2 Deck, way above the waterline. He was amazed to see water rushing past his port!

The Captain would later add: "It looked as if we were going straight into the White Cliffs of Dover!"

Visually, and from data gleaned from Canadian weather monitors in the area, the wave had been from 95 to 98-feet in height and around 1,200-feet wide. Railings around the foredeck had been buckled and the deck plating of the tip of the foredeck had been buckled downwards to show the lines of the beams and longitudinal stiffening underneath.

As June Applebee summed up her feelings: " ...An amazing experience to have been on board....*QE2* is an amazing ship and one feels confident in any situation that the elements care to throw at her" - a sentiment echoed by everybody on board from the Master downwards.

Storm Certificates were issued the next day as a memento.

By going through that ordeal the *Queen Elizabeth 2* proved herself to the press and, in the waters of the rogue wave, seemed to slough the bad feelings generated by her December refit. Once again she was Queen of the Seas.

Above: The liner positioned on the Blomm + Voss floating dock at Hamburg during her 1994 refit.
Below: A splendid painting of the *Queen Elizabeth 2* surrounded by fleets of racing yachts off Cowes.

Harley Crossley
Painting by Robert Lloyd

Chapter Twenty Three

Sailing On

"**M**editerranean Medley" was the title of the cruise that left Southampton on 15th October, 1995. Barcelona was the first stop-over followed by Villefranche, Genoa, Palma, Gibraltar and Lisbon. What made this cruise so particular to many British people was that many of the cast from the top-rating television soap "Coronation Street" were on board to film a Christmas special. Curly, Rita, Alec, Raquel, *et al* performed their stuff but it appeared that it was filmed mostly late at night as the spacious but normally busy *QE2* seemed strangely deserted in the final film. Members of the cast have often travelled on the ship as part of the on-board entertainment talking to passengers and giving autographs.

At the beginning of 1996 Cunard announced that they had received a record number of bookings for the year in spite of, or probably because of, the adverse publicity stemming from the so-called "Christmas Cruise From Hell"!

It was all too late for Trafalgar House. Heavy losses over the previous year and a recent stranding and fire on the *Sagafjord* led them finally to accepting a bid from the Norwegian construction and engineering group of Kvaerner and, in March, Trafalgar was sold for £904-million. At first it was thought that, although Kvaerner appeared to be happy with the cruising side of the business, Cunard might be sold on. The collision of their super-luxury *Royal Viking Sun* with a Red Sea coral reef probably did nothing to make them change their minds. Kvaerner's chief executive said bluntly: "Cunard falls outside our core business". But it was later announced officially that Cunard was not for sale although Carnival, P&O and Sea Containers expressed interest. Cunard was valued at above £200-million but would need a substantial investment if Kvaerner could not sell it. Cunard's London address was moved to Berkeley Street.

At the same time, as seems to be periodically usual, there were rumours that the *QE2's* base would be moved from Southampton either to America or Japan. This rumour was based on a fall in *QE2* profits over recent years and it was felt that a more lucrative base market could be found where the ships great reputation could be exploited.

It was whilst she was on her 1996 World Cruise - her twentieth - that another milestone was reached in the story of the remakable *Queen Elizabeth 2*: or rather her four-

The *Queen* in the spectacular setting of Invergordon during her inaugural call there at the developing cruise port.

Courtesy of Cromarty Firth Port Authority

QE2 in the Geiranger Fjord, Norway, in 1999. The other two liners are the *Maxim Gorky* and *Black Prince*. The Cunarder's anchor went down a long way!   *Len and Margaret Thompson*

A brace of handsome Cunarders together off Barbados. *Queen Elizabeth 2* and *Caronia* met again at the turn of the Millenium.   *Cunard*

The 1996 refit was carried out, after an absence of several years, in Southampton. The structural work that was carried out included the removal and relacement of the bow plates buckled after the liner's encounter with a 90 foot wave! The discarded piece of fore deck can be seen on the edge of the King George V dry dock where the work was carried out.

millionth-milestone! An extraordinary achievement.

During the time that the company she belonged to was being sold to a non-British owner the *Queen Elizabeth 2* was still on her 1996 World Cruise. Entitled "Voyage to Distant Empires" it lasted from 4th January (New York) to 8th April (New York) and, as usual, segments of the voyage were sold as shorter cruises (fares from $24,230 each for an inside cabin sharing to $537,800 for each of the Queen Mary/Queen Elizabeth suites for the whole cruise).

Beating off fierce competition it was announced in May that the Southampton ship-repair firm of A&P Southampton (part of the A&P Group) had won the bid to refit the *Queen* during the coming December with a £12-million contract. Southampton was jubilant, realising again how important this ship was to the city.

1996 turned out to be a remarkably uneventful year for the *Queen Elizabeth 2*. No doubt, her owners were glad of this and it gave the ship time to renew her old popularity.

Some family nostalgia was commemorated in a special transatlantic and Bermudan cruise to recall the sixtieth anniversary of the maiden voyage of perhaps the most famous ocean liner ever - the *Queen Mary*. 18th May saw *QE2's* departure from Southampton celebrating that famous, historical voyage that had captured the imagination of the world.

The American "leg" of this cruise took the *QE2* to Bermuda and she was booked to capacity - there was even a waiting list! In what would be described as "...one of the most exciting and successful cruises in recent years...", the trip had all the right ingredients for a trip of nostalgia: good weather, a beautiful destination, good rates and a ship full of ocean liner enthusiasts from various shipping societies and museums.

The day to Bermuda and the day returning were filled with lectures by noted maritime authors John Maxton-Graham and Bill Miller, and displays - and sales - of memorabilia were provided by Richard Faber in the Boardroom. Captain Warwick's only chance of seeing the displays and to avoid a lengthy queue was to find his way through the Queen's Grill kitchen! The *QE2's* own new Heritage Trail was also eagerly explored.

On 5th August, during a "Northern Capitals" cruise, the *Queen* assumed a fifty-foot dent after breaking free of her tugs in Copenhagen and ramming the quay wall. A September cruise to the Iberian Peninsula that had been scheduled in the brochure for 1996 had been cancelled almost as soon as the brochure had been issued. One hundred early bookers had refunds or the chance to take a cruise of greater value plus generous compensation. The liner had been chartered for £1-million to act as a floating hotel during the Ryder Cup golf tournament which was held at Valderrame, near Cadiz.

Prince Edward was once again on board QE2 (28th September) hosting another Royal Ball in aid of his father's

Special Projects Group, which was celebrating its tenth anniversary. Tickets cost up to £300 and the entertainment included supper, a fireworks display and plenty of music. The partying finished at 4am.

Bizarrely, in September, the ship rammed and killed a whale, an event not unknown at sea as the *Caronia* had similarly done so off the East African coast in 1958.

Kvaerner finally admitted in November that they were intending to sell their interests in Cunard (the company had lost £16.5-million in 1995) but it would be several months before negotiations were completed and a buyer could be announced.

The big refit of 1996 started on 21st November and the *Queen Elizabeth 2* was dry-docked in the King George V Graving Dock, the first time for nine years, that had been built to accommodate the *Queen Mary* during her annual overhauls. A&P (Southampton), who were chosen to undertake the work against stiff competition, had to temporarily increase their workforce from their normal 130 to 1,000.

Over the previous three months the company had already refitted the *Black Prince*, *Black Watch* and the mighty *Norway* (ex-*France*) that had made a special North Atlantic voyage of nostalgia to travel to Southampton for her refit. Amongst the work to be done on the *QE2* was to finish forty-three top grade bathrooms (marble and gold in best art deco style) that remained to be completed after her last refit and refurbish several public rooms as well as 160 cabins. Passenger capacity would again be reduced, this time to fifteen hundred giving more space per passenger and reducing sittings to one in the Mauretania Restaurant.

In anticipation of new SOLAS (Safety Of Life At Sea) regulations that would be coming into force the following year, four thousand fire and smoke detection devices were also fitted. This equipment (including detectors, interface modules and call-points) linked to controllers placed in the Wheelhouse and safety centre. Mimic displays were installed to give a clear indication of which call points on the ship were in alarm. Fire doors on crew stairways were also refitted and the remaining asbestos was removed. Other technical work included propellers, stabilisers, the overhaul and replacement where necessary of five miles of pipework, classification society survey of anchors and chains, hull blasting and repainting, etc. The work was completed on time and to budget.

Other work included the fitting of a new six-inch thick, English Oak, sprung dance floor in the Queen's Room, replacing the original that had been there for nearly thirty years. A new foredeck section replaced the area of buckled deck that remained as a souvenir of Hurricane "Luis". The Mauretania Restaurant, an increasingly attractive room with new lighting and a new suspended glass-fibre ceiling, had its seating capacity increased to cater for a single sitting and the telegraph from the first *Mauretania* was moved to the entrance of the officers' Wardroom. The One Deck branch of Harrod's was changed to a Gift shop, later becoming the "Cunard Collection Shop".

Both the Queen Mary and Queen Elizabeth suites were enlarged being extended to incorporate the adjacent cabins which became new bedrooms and dining rooms with six chairs.

Veteran of 38 *QE2* cruises, Sir Jimmy Savile, had been given a special tour of the ship on 4th December whilst she was still in dry-dock. Impressed with what he saw he told the local Southampton "Daily Echo": "She is like a relative to me so I have come to see how she is getting on. I can't wait to get back on board afterwards. In fact, I might just stow away on the next cruise!"

After the experiences suffered after the 1994 refit A&P and the hard-working ship's staff ensured that the ship, was "spic-and-span" by the time that passengers boarded on 12th December in readiness for a three-day party cruise. These three days would either prove the ship or they could be cancelled to allow any outstanding work that was required to be completed. As it was, A&P had finished ahead of time which allowed the high standard of preparedness in readiness to embark passengers to be achieved and sea trials were carried out on the 11th. Relief Captain Keith Stanley was justifiably proud of his ship as he showed the shipping press around his vessel.

After the three-day party cruise a transatlantic (these were now scheduled to take six instead of five days) was followed by a Caribbean Christmas Cruise returning to New York for the start of the 1997 World Cruise leaving the city on 4th January under the command of John Burton-Hall who was making his last round-the-world cruise before retiring.

When the *Queen* called at Hong Kong she embarked sixteen government officers and seventeen dependants. This would be the liner's last call there before mainland China took over the British colony. The *QE2* had always been looked after in Hong Kong, receiving a mid-world cruise paint "make-over" there and even appearing on one of the colony's postage stamps.

The cruise during its final stages from 21st March, was also sold as smaller cruise segments, the longest being as the *Queen Elizabeth 2* made her maiden call into Dubai (in the United Arab Emirates) which was hoping to develop into a cruise ship centre. Fly/cruise passengers could join her here on her westward "Odyssey Through the Ancient World". The liner was met in the Strait of Hormuz by HMS *Southampton*, then on the Armilla Patrol in the Persian Gulf, which escorted the *Queen* into port.

1997 bought in a change to the transatlantic voyages. In future they would include six nights at sea instead of the more hectic five as before. This was partly due to passenger demand but it would also save Cunard the cost of the oil-fuel used in high-speed crossings and would also provide a "cushion" for any delays (caused, for example, by inclement weather) thereby giving an allowance in which, if necessary, to make up lost time.

In mid-March Kvaerner's chairman, Antti Pankakoski, spoke about the possibility of building a running mate for the *QE2* but the company would no longer own Cunard by the time that such a decision would be made. Peter Ward had resigned in September, taking with him any threat to remove the Heritage Trail; his position as President would be taken the following June by Captain Paris Katsoufis.

Arriving home in Southampton on the morning of 11th April the *Queen Elizabeth 2* sailed the next day at noon on a 22-day Spring circular tour of the Atlantic. On board she carried the ashes of the late Commodore of the Cunard Line, Geoffrey Marr, one-time captain of the fabled *Queens* as well as of the *Caronia*, *Mauretania*, etc, for committing to the deep waters of the North Atlantic on 14th April. Relief Captain Roland Hassel officiated with Chief Officer Ian McNaught in attendance. After a remarkable career - which had included witnessing the sinking of the German battleship *Bismark* from an advantageous point on *HMS King George V* - the Commodore had lived in retirement at Redlynch in the New Forest (where he had written his eminently readable "The Queens And I"). A move to Devizes preceeded a lengthy transfer to his daughter's farm in Scotland. He had been taken ill whilst visiting his son near London and had spent his last days in the Royal Alfred Home For Sailors in Surrey. Away from his old friends that he missed in and around the New Forest there were very few at his funeral.

On 11th April too, rather strangely and inexplicably, the Mauretania and Caronia Restaurants were swapped around (the Mauretania was reinstated back to where it used to be pre-1994). The name boards around the entrances were the only items to be exchanged in the exercise whilst the *QE2* was alongside her Southampton terminal. The *Caronia* model, painting and mural remained where they were in the Upper Deck restaurant as did the horse sculpture and fountain. The large model of the *Mauretania* remained outside what now became the Caronia Restaurant. This anomaly could never be explained to the curious enquirer.

"Where on Earth will you be at midnight on December 31st, 1999?" was the question already being posed by Cunard's publicists in advance material issued for the Millenium. Discounts, as usual, were being

offered on bookings taken in advance. The *Queen's* new millenium would be spent, it was said, in Barbados.

The *QE2* settled down to her varied and very busy schedule and thankfully remained free of any major negative occurences that would have caused instant press reaction.

July 1997 marked a major event when the British dependent territory of Hong Kong was reverted back into Chinese Sovereignty. But this favourite amongst the ports of call during her world cruises (usually staying there for a lengthy three days at the beginning of March during each world cruise) would still remain on her future itineraries. Hong Kong now came under the care of the son of C Y Tung (T'ung Chao Yung), the man who had bought the venerable old '*Lizzie*', converting her into a floating university, Seawise University. The old ship on the brink of a new lease of life burnt out and capsized just prior to her entering service in 1970. She was broken up on the spot. Tung Chee Hwa, CY's son, would become Chief Executive, Hong Kong Special Administrative Region Peoples' Republic of China, when the old British colony was returned to the Chinese Government. Some had taken the *QE2*'s final trip to Hong Kong prior to the handover before 'they' took over but the liner would continue to use the port in the years that followed.

Top: A captain's view of the Bridge of the Americas, Panama Canal.
Cunard

Left: The names of the Caronia and Mauretania Restaurants were inexplicably transposed even though artifacts relating to the liners after whom the restaurants were named remained where they stood! Here the Mauretania Restaurant is being renamed Caronia - and not as an honour to Captain Ron Warwick!
Author

In August westbound the ship missed a call at Cobh on the 8th because of fog leaving some passengers stranded (which caused a mild disturbance in the lurking press). Some of the disappointed passengers prefered the enforced wait for the ship's next call on the 25th rather than fly. On arrival the *QE2* sailed from New York to spend two nights anchored off Newport, Rhode Island, during that towns famous Jazz Festival.

Later the *Queen* hosted a special group of people that provided one of the many theme cruises that Cunard regularly organise. The transatlantic westbound from Southampton that began on 24th August carried a group of thirty of the worlds top chefs, many of them in the service of world leaders. Called "Le Club des Chefs des Chefs" they were hosted by Cunard's Executive Chef, Rudi Sodamin. The passengers dined with an even greater luxury and variety on the trip.

At the end of August Cunard relocated its worldwide corporate headquarters from 555 Fifth Avenue, New York (which it had occupied for many years) to Dade County in

An upward drift of 1,159 balloons (one for each voyage) hastened by a brisk breeze colorfully speckle the sky at the start of the liner's 30th Birthday celebratory voyage to New York. *Mick Lindsey*

Miami, Florida (it was rumoured that this was done because the Chief executive lived in that area!) As a result the Cunard fleet switched from using Port Everglades to the Port of Miami. The new port of call was inaugurated by the *QE2* on her visit on 15th November which meant a change in her published schedule.

The *Queen Elizabeth 2* has carried the rich and the famous and the prominent during her sea-going career but on 7th August she sailed from Southampton carrying a lady whose claim to fame lay elsewhere and who had not been on the Atlantic - or even on a large ship - for eighty-five years. At nine weeks old she had disembarked in New York, carried by her mother and accompanied by her elder brother Bertram, from the Cunard liner *Carpathia*. Little Millvina Dean had left Southampton on 10th April 1912, with her family headed by her father. The ship on which they sailed towards a new life in America that never materialised was the *Titanic* and Millvina, the youngest survivor of that tragedy, was now going to the States as the principal guest of the Titanic Historical Society.

A rare photograph of the Cunard liner *Carpathia* of 1903 in dry-dock. It was this 13,500-ton liner that made a gallant dash on the morning of 15th April 1912, to rescue the survivors from the White Star liner *Titanic*.
Collection of the Author

At the end of the month, on 31st August, the United Kingdom and the world had been stunned at the news from Paris that Diana, Princess of Wales had died as a result of a car accident. Two minutes silence was held on the *QE2* which was westbound for New York. The following month a special luncheon was held on the ship in aid of the British Red Cross campaign against landmines, a cause in which the late Princess had an abiding interest, still went ahead on 1st October both in memory of the Princess and as part of the liner's celebrations of the thirtieth anniversary of her own launching.

The Princess had been due to attend the fund raising lunch (for which 300 people had paid £350 per ticket) which was also attended by Lord Richard Attenborough; former hostage Terry Waite; Elizabeth Dole (President of the American branch of the Red Cross); and Cherie Blair (wife of the British Prime Minister). The guests were greeted by Captain Ron Warwick and £70,000 was raised from the occasion. Cunard's Chief Executive, Antti Pankakoski, also announced that the Red Cross would become the company's official charity until the year 2000.

Helping to celebrate the liner's anniversary the *QE2's* Grill Class accommodation was awarded, in September, a Five-star accolade by the "Berlitz Complete Guide to Cruising and Cruise Ships", becoming Number One in the large ship category.

20th September saw celebrations on board *Queen Elizabeth 2* during Voyage 1,104 *en-route* for Southampton in honour of the actual anniversary of her launching.

Meanwhile, negotiations were quietly continuing between Kvaerner and agents, the ship-owning and managing Vlasov Group of Monaco, for the sale of the Cunard once again, this time to an as yet undiclosed buyer.

An American Thanksgiving cruise left New York on 13th November for a 9th December return, turning around at Los Angeles on 26th November. Thanksgiving, 27th November, was spent at sea. Before joining the ship at LA passengers had lunch on board the old *Queen Mary*, permanently berthed in retirement at Long Beach. There were two attractions on this particular cruise: a double transition of the Panama Canal and the presence on board of American comedian and actor Bill Cosby.

The ship returned to Southampton on 15th December prior to her depature for New York at the outset of her World Cruise, "Exploration of Distant Lands", that took her to Pacific islands, New Zealand, Australia, Japan, China (Hong Kong), Vietnam, Singapore, Indonesia, India, Africa and around the Horn to Portugal, arriving back in Southampton on 15th April, 1998. It was on this cruise that retired Captain and Mrs Robin Woodall fulfilled one of his ambitions for retirement - to sail on his beloved old command as passengers!

During *QE2's* call in to Durban, South Africas President, Nelson Mandela, boarded the liner and journeyed with her to Cape Town. A luncheon was held on board during this voyage around the Horn of Africa in aid of The Nelson Mandela Childrens Fund. Also during the trip the President was interviewed during a live televised broadcast by David Frost for his programme "Breakfast With Frost". Mr Mandela unveiled a plaque to commemorate his visit before leaving the ship.

Whilst the *Queen Elizabeth 2* was completing her World Cruise it was announced that Kvaerner had sold its interests in Cunard to a joint venture between Norwegian investors holding 32% and the mighty Carnival Corporation (68%) of Miami. Exciting plans were unveiled for the new company (Cunard Line Limited) after its merger with Carnival. Seabourn Cruise Line would join with Cunard with *QE2* and *Vistafjord* (to be renamed *Caronia*) being British flagged and officered whilst the Seabourne ships (*Seabourn Goddess(es) I* and *II* - ex-*Sea Goddess(es) I* and *II* - and *Seabourn Sun*, ex-*Royal Viking Sun*) would similarly be Norwegian registered. The British government had recently at long last decided that the country's merchant fleet had dwindled to unacceptable levels and were providing tax concessions to companies to re-flag their fleets. *QE2*, however, already flew the Red (or Blue) Ensign and in herself made up a large proportion of the British fleet.

Not only was a corporate indentity to be given to the Cunard ships by using a recognisable livery (and the traditional naming suffix of "...ia" in Cunard's case) in each component company but ambitious plans for a new ship were announced in June. This would be for the biggest, most expensive transatlantic liner ever to be built and was given the project name of "Project *Queen Mary*". An unique feature of the new 150,000gt ship would be the proposed inclusion of privately-owned apartments on board for the mega-rich!

Larry Pimentel, Cunard's new president, said: "The project will lead to the development of the grandest and largest liner ever built - the epitome of elegance, style and grace.

"It is our objective to build a new generation of ocean liner that will be the very pinnacle of the shipbuilders' art; the realisation of a dream of another time. Our goal is nothing less than to create a new Golden Age of Sea Travel for those who missed the first!"

Early artists' impressions of the proposed new *Queen Mary* showed a vessel larger but not dissimilar to the *QE2*. This would be the first new-building for Cunard for many years and the exciting news was welcomed by observers who had noted that Cunard, unlike its competitors who commissioned new ships, had relied on "taken-over" tonnage for far too long. Cunard's short-lived headquarters in Blue Lagoon Drive, Miami, would also be moved again, this time to Fort Lauderdale.

Meantime, the *QE2* carried on with a transatlantic return voyage that preceded a 16-night cruise to Istanbul and back. Caribbean and Baltic cruises followed and on 19th July, at the end of a return from New York, the *Queen Elizabeth 2* anchored in beautiful Falmouth Bay to allow her passengers to see the start of the 1998 "Cutty Sark" Tall Ships Race. After three hours of the parade of sail passing the huge liner the *QE2* followed the race for a further three hours.

Another popular "Round Britain Discovery" cruise was operated in August with the *Queen* again sailing clockwise around the UK.

October brought two revelations in the press. Firstly, that a wealthy businessman had been booking the top two suites for himself and his wife on world cruises for the past eight years (along with other staterooms for their luggage!) and that a special book had been planned about the ship. The top edition of a mere thirty copies was soon sold out. This would have a bejewelled cover by Asprey's of London and would cost £25,000! Other editions would have a silver porthole as its cover motif (nearly £600); another edition at almost £250 and an 'edition *ordinaire*' at less than £20! The author of the planned book would be Carol Thatcher, journalist daughter of the late Prime Minister, who had given lectures aboard the ship on previous voyages.

1998 ended with the traditional Caribbean christmas cruise terminating in New York on 5th January, 1999.

Chapter Twenty Four

For Sale - or Good for Thirty Years?

The New Year would prove to be an important one for the *Queen Elizabeth 2*. Her World Cruise (£18,770 to £193,410 for the complete 99-days) started from New York on 5th January and finished in Southampton on 14th April. Since the introduction of her six-day transatlantic schedule the *Queen* was always timed for a 7am arrival in Southampton (although this was more usually 6am) and the same stood for her return from World Cruises. A 5pm sailing invariably (bar delays) followed.

Terminal in Southampton docks were not in the least bit dampened. Several ex-*Queen Elizabeth 2* captains were present for this most unusual but joyful event including Peter Jackson, Robin Woodall, Bob Arnott, Douglas Ridley, Mortimer Heier, Lawrence Portet and Keith Stanley. Captain Roland Hassel was also in attendance as was Ron Warwick as the Senior Captain. Unhappily Ron Warwick's father, retired Captain 'Bil' Warwick, had been due to attend but his death, at 86, had occured only a few weeks before the

Surrounded by a festive throng the 30-year old *QE2* sails from Southampton *en-route* to New York.   *Author*

14th April commemorated two notable shipping events. The 'big one' was the anniversary of the White Star liner *Titanic* striking an iceberg in 1912 that led to her foundering with great loss of life in the early hours of the following morning. The second event, in 1999, was the celebration in Southampton of the *Queen Elizabeth 2's* thirtieth anniversary of her maiden voyage. Although the actual anniversary would not be until 2nd May it had been decided to hold her birthday party in her home port on the day that she arrived home from her World Cruise.

The party day stated in a typically changeable manner for April - cloudy, rain, sleet and lightning - but the spirits of those joining *QE2* alongside the Queen Elizabeth II

event. A few moments silence during the on-board presentation would be held in his memory.

Many famous personalities from British show business and the media were also present, representing the hundreds of top name people who had lectured on board the ship at some time in the past. Those fortunate few, numbering less than five hundred, who were on board to mark the *QE2*'s special anniversary were given a presentation by Larry Pimentel, Cunard's new president under the Carnival Corporation, and he spoke of Carnival's plans for the line's future. The fabulous 'Project *Queen Mary*' was not only officially launched but plans for a second such vessel were also announced as were plans for a major £19-million refit for the *QE2* which would take place later in the year, giving her and the 'new' *Caronia* (ex-*Vistafjord*) a corporate identity in company livery. Mr Pimentel said, 'we are very proud to own this ship, and very well aware of its place as a national institution and the affection it holds throughout the world'.

After the presentation a large cake depicting the *QE2* was wheeled onto the stage and Captains Ron Warwick and Roland Hassel (standing in for 'Bil' Warwick) made the first cut.

After lunch in the Caronia Restaurant (during which each guest was presented with a copy of Gary Buchanan's superbly illustrated '*QE2 - A Magnificent Millennium*' which photographically traced the various internal alterations that the ship had undergone). *QE2*'s famous fan, Sir Jimmy Saville, spoke on behalf of the guests and proposed the well-deserved toast to the *Queen Elizabeth 2*.

During the afternoon the inclement weather abated leaving a sunny but blustery, Spring afternoon in its wake. At 5pm the *QE2* pulled away from her berth as 1,159 red, white and blue balloons were released, peppering the sky with pin-pricks of colour, each balloon representing a voyage made during her 4.5-million miles of ocean travel. The liner then sounded thirty blasts on her siren as the tugs around her sent tapering plumes of water upwards into the air with apparently much of Southampton Water apparently landing on the liner as a result! Meanwhile, spectators both on shore and on the myriad of small craft surrounding the liner cheered and waved the *QE2* yet another *Bon Voyage* as she sailed for the United States. She arrived in New

York to be greeted by the press and a glorious gold and red sunrise six days later.

Associated British Ports had placed a full-page advert in a special *QE2* anniversary supplement of the Southampton 'Daily Echo' proclaiming 'Many Happy Returns *QE2*' and showing a photograph of the ship with thirty superimposed pink candles alight on her superstructure. A few months later, in October, ABP and Cunard were involved in their almost traditional three-yearly joust about the 'high costs' of berthing fees. The Cunard as per usual, threatened to take *QE2* away from the port and a vigorous campaign ensued in the Southampton paper to keep the ship in the city. The campaign appeared to be successful with Cunard even committing to using the Port of Southampton for their prestigious new *Queen Mary 2*.

Another of *QE2*'s milestones another was reached on Sunday 13th June whilst *en-route* between Southampton and Madeira. The ship's siren was sounded to mark twenty years - or 175,296 hours - of actual steaming time, making the *Queen Elizabeth 2* the hardest working vessel in the history of the Cunard Line.

In stark contrast to the celebrations of 1999 it was revealed from recently released papers that Cunard had barely survived the upheavals that it had faced in the mid-sixties. It was also revealed that it was even contemplated

Left: A huge cake representing the *QE2* was wheeled onto stage during the on-board celebrations in Southampton and ceremoniously cut by Captains Ron Warwick and Roland Hassle.

Below: During the Millennium World Cruise the *Queen Elizabeth 2* met the recently renamed *Caronia* (ex-*Vistafjord*) off Barbados.

Cunard

that the company might be liquidated and the then new *Queen Elizabeth 2* sold after her launch in 1967, perhaps to a Greek shipping company. However, in August 1969, the magazine 'Shipbuilding and Shipping Record' quoted Lord Mancroft, then Cunard's deputy chairman as publicly giving an assurance that '....the ship would be remaining under Cunard's flag throughout her career, estimated to be 27 to 30 years'. He also commented on the fact that a number of people had been worried about the prospect of the ship being sold to P&O or to an American company, especially in view of the sale of her predecessors, but these worries were unfounded.

QE2 followed her usual cruise pattern for the rest of the year and her pilgrimage to the North Cape in July almost following those similar cruises undertaken by her illustrious predecessor, the *Caronia*, during the fifties by including several UK and Irish ports in her itinerary.

The British mercantile marine that had been in decline for many years was given a fillip in August 1999 when the British Deputy Prime Minister, John Prescott, (himself an ex-steward on board liners such as *Caronia* and *Queen Mary* and staunch union member and official), introduced tax concessions for shipowners. This action attempted in some way to undo some of the severe damage that his old union had caused the merchant navy in 1966 when he had personally assisted in the great Seamens' Strike by, amongst other actions, exhorting fellow seamen on board the *Queen Mary* to walk off the ship on strike. The Strike, which crippled British sea trade, would eventually bring about the virtual collapse of Britain as a seafaring nation.

Now, with the new concessions, shipowners were encouraged to recommence training future seamen and thus help to alleviate an impending world shortage. The *QE2*, until now by far the largest vessel to fly the Red Ensign under British registry, was joined by fifty units of the mighty P&O fleet. The presence of the Red Ensign upon the oceans of the world was practically doubled in a very short time. Britannia had started to regain her lost crown.

On Trafalgar Day, 21st October, the Carnival Corporation wholly acquired the Cunard. They thereby achieved what their fellow Americans had failed to do at the turn of the century when financier J. Pierpoint Morgan's giant International Mercantile Marine Company was taking over many North Atlantic shipping companies, including Cunard's arch-rival - the White Star Line. The world-wide fame of Cunard's long and often distinguished history, now the jewel in Carnival's crown, would later be lauded in 'corporate-speak' by the new owners as 'global brand equity'

On her arrival in Southampton on 10th November from a Panama and Caribbean cruise the *QE2* disembarked her passengers and sailed for her promised £19.5-million refit. This again would be undertaken at the German Bremerhaven yard of Lloyd Werft which was also refitting the *Royal Viking Sun* (to be renamed *Seabourn Sun*) and the *Vistafjord*, shortly to be renamed *Caronia*.

Whilst in Bremerhaven the liner became the target of protest by the environmental group Greenpeace. In common with many hundreds of other ships the *QE2*'s underwater hull was painted with an anti-fouling paint that had, as a chemical biocide, a high tin content known as tributyltin (TBT). This effectively prevented algae and molluscs from growing on ships' hulls, thus slowing them down and increasing fuel bills. It also prevented undesirable foreign marine life from being spread from one world location to another. Equally, it was a toxic pollutant, released when water blasted during hull cleaning as well as by erosion due

to its self-polishing capabilities. The pollution persisted in water and had become a prime concern as it killed sealife, harmed the environment and possibly entered the food chain.

To make their protest against TBT Greenpeace had chosen their world-famous target well. A flotilla of small inflatable craft sped around the ship as she sailed through Bremerhaven harbour and fifty protesters dived into the water to prevent the vessel from moving forward or astern. Two hundred other protesters waved banners that proclaimed 'Stop TBT!' and the crew of one inflatable drew up alongside the towering hull and spray-painted 'God Save the *Queen* from TBT' along her hull just above the waterline.

The protest worked as Cunard officials gave an assurance that TBT-based paints would no longer be used on the *QE2* nor on any of their other ships.

Since then the International Maritime Organisation (IMO), the maritime regulatory body of the United Nations, has put into its agenda a suggestion that TBT based paints should not be used after 1st January 2003 and that hulls painted with the deadly organotins should be repainted or sealed by 1st January 2008. More acceptable coatings would be recommended such as a silicon rubber compound that provides a 'non-stick' surface that allows marine growth to attach itself to a ship's bottom but is then washed off once the vessel is underway.

Over the next month the *QE2* would undergo the third most important refit of her life and one that would establish her place amongst the vanguard of the world fleet of liners and cruise ships. £12-million would be spent on her redecoration brilliantly masterminded by Tillberg Design whilst £7.5-million would be expended on the technical aspects of the work.

New carpets, furnishings, decor, lighting and re-upholstery would enhance the three grillrooms. The Mauretania Restaurant would receive new furnishings and carpets as well as chandeliers and new glass doors and the *Caronia* mural was replaced with one depicting a lily pond at evening which seemed to reflect the warm tones of the room's furnishings. The Caronia Restaurant was redesigned to create an '.... English country house feel'. Mahogany panelling and mahogany encased pillars and beams that highlighted a white ceiling would recall the elegance of the earlier Edwardian steamers. New lighting, including chandeliers, carpets, curtains and chairs along with an enhanced music system made the room into a superb dining area. Anomalies still existed between the themes of the two restaurants that perhaps provided the only discordant note of the whole refit.

The Queen's Room received new furniture and a luxurious carpet in royal blue with a woven motif of Tudor roses in gold. Mahogany panelling was applied to the bulkheads. Oscar Nemon's bust of HM The Queen was prominently relocated. Unfortunately it still retained its heavy gold leafing and had not been returned to its original *vert-de-gris* finish. The Grand Lounge received a new stage, chairs, curtains and carpet and the Theatre and balcony were rejuvenated with new upholstery and carpeting. Stairs were no longer evident in the Lounge, thus creating more useful space.

The Yacht Club, Chart Room, Crystal Bar and Golden Lion pub were all modified during the refit and 106 bathrooms were renewed to complete the work commenced in 1994. New luxury suites were created or enlarged and given - or renamed with - the names of historical Cunarders, thus maintaining the ship's theme of company heritage. One

The longest and the last of the ocean liners designed and built for the North Atlantic run meet in their cruising capacities in Miami. The *Norway* (ex-*France*) had long been converted from her liner role to one of cruising.

Richard Weiss

of the new suites, the Caledonia (575 square feet) on the Boat Deck, had been built using space formerly occupied by the Radio Room. The arrival of GMDSS had helped to obviate the requirement for such a large room and a new, compact, communications centre was located in the Purser's Office on 2 Deck. Corridors and stairways around the ship were also refurbished with new wall coverings and carpets.

As a welcome return to traditional comforts - and perhaps influenced by the recent blockbuster movie 'Titanic' - the *QE2*'s deck furniture was replaced with new teak-wood steamer chairs of classic design.

Externally the *Queen* had been given the new, almost traditional, Cunard livery. Her hull had been blasted to remove the accumulation and weight of fifty-two layers of paint. The Trafalgar House 'Go-faster' stripe disappeared from the superstructure as did the quite attractive golden lion at the line's forward end above the legend 'CUNARD'. The Trafalgar House emblem of signal flags astern of the stripe had disappeared previously when Kvaerner had taken control of the Line.

It is planned at some future overhaul to completely clear the aluminium superstructure of its old layers of paint and perhaps repair the athwartships cracks forward of the funnel and over the Queen's Grill. The latter crack has been problematical, as it has at various times seeped water on to the diners below. A temporary solution has been to fit some grey household guttering below the split to drain away such unwelcome water!

At the outset of the refit Larry Pimentel had said: 'This refit is the first stage of an overall master-plan we are developing for *QE2*. The ship has a long life ahead of her and we are committed to maintaining, and improving even further, the already high standards for which she is known'.

Arriving back in Southampton on 9th December the *Queen Elizabeth 2* sailed on a three-day shakedown cruise entitled 'Pre-Millennium Celebration'. On her return to Southampton early on the morning of Sunday 12th December the *Queen* was made ready to welcome her companion in the Cunard Line, the 'new' *Caronia*.

The *Caronia* had been re-named as such at a

spectacular ceremony in Liverpool the previous Friday and had sailed south with a group of very special guests - Lord Lichfield (the Queen's cousin) amongst them, personalities (including many characters from television programmes such as 'Coronation Street' and 'Keeping Up Appearances') and journalists (Jenny Bond, Sir Michael Ingram, Michael Buerk, etc,) on board. A Force 9 in the Irish Sea had been encountered (laying many of the passengers low) but this had reduced in its effect as the liner turned into the English Channel. On arrival at Southampton her passengers were taken to the *Queen Elizabeth 2* that lay ahead of her to inspect the larger liner's new interiors.

A special celebratory luncheon was held for them, appropriately in the Caronia Restaurant, during which a *QE2* cookbook was presented to the ladies and a copy of Captain Ron Warwick's own magnificent volume, '*QE2*', was given to the gentlemen.

The thirty-year old liner, rejuvenated and redesigned over several major refits was now looking her magnificent best.

And so the *Queen Elizabeth 2* had achieved what had been wished for her (and only a few could have realistically hoped for realisation) in her early and subsequent years - both her thirtieth year of service in the Cunard and to sail into a New Millennium.

The liner sailed the same day for New York on the outset of her Millennium World Cruise entitled 'Circling the Water Planet' (fares from £14,550 to £153,030 per person for the full sixty-nine days). Arriving and departing from New York on 18th December the *QE2* circumnavigated the globe from west to east, again rounding the Cape of Good Hope at the southern tip of Africa before heading north for Southampton via St. Helena, Agadir and Lisbon. Maiden calls were often made during the World Cruises and during this cruise the *QE2* made maiden calls at Zihuatanejo in Mexico; Port Douglas, Australia; Madang in Papua, New Guinea and at Pointe des Galets on the Indian Ocean island of Reunion. New Year's Eve for the year 2000 had been spent at Bridgetown on the Caribbean island of Barbados where she met up with the *Caronia* on her maiden Caribbean cruise.

4th July, Independence Day, 2000 saw the Cunarder being eased into her berth in New York after providing a grandstand view of a three-day spectacular maritime event during which time the *QE2* had been anchored. In a high wind and with adjacent berths crowded with ships that had taken part in the festival the liner was being assisted out of her dock when the three tugs accompanying her momentarily lost control causing the ship's stern to veer ultimately colliding with a Japanese National Defence vessel, the *Kashima*. Just prior to the collision a startled Japanese sailor rushed to the impending collision point, hastily lowering a small, plastic fender over his ship's side! The collision caused the loss of paint on both ships and a buckled rail on the *QE2*. As a reaction to the collision the *Kashima*'s mooring ropes snapped and sent her forward to collide with the British destroyer, HMS *Manchester*!

Officers from *Queen Elizabeth 2* later went aboard the Japanese vessel to make their peace with their counterparts but were told that 'It had been an honour to be kissed by such gracious a lady!'

The *Queen*'s own damaged paintwork was soon repaired by a painting party lowered over her side.

There have been many that, taken by flights of fancy, have tried to stow away on the *Queen* with varying degrees of success. Not least are the many birds, some rare, which have settled on the liner's decks to rest in mid-flight only to find themselves transported many miles away from their intended destinations. In July, 2001, a pair of racing pigeons settled down to rest on the ship during a foggy race from France to England and subsequently found themselves *en-route* for New York. Taken into care on board the liner the birds sailed to the Caribbean via New York and back before being reunited with their owners in Southampton in a flurry of publicity.

The oft-times consort of the *Queen Elizabeth 2*, the sleek, supersonic Concorde (originally specially chartered but later used on scheduled flights), also celebrated its 30th Anniversary in 1999. But, on 25th July, 2000, one of the aircraft belonging to Air France suffered a catastrophic tragedy on take-off from Paris' Charles de Gaulle airport. A piece of debris on the runway ruptured the aircraft's starboard wing fuel tank, causing the plane to catch fire and crash with the tragic loss of 109 lives. The Concordes of both the British and French fleets were

One of the super-luxury suites. The *QE2* boasts her own butler to serve the de-luxe accommodations.

Cunard

withdrawn from service for sixteen months whilst improved safety features were built into their fuel tanks. Much improved, the aircraft were reintroduced into service during November, 2001. Concorde and *QE2* were soon to offer a joint service to create once again 'the ultimate transatlantic travel experience.'

An eastwards September 2000 sailing headed the *QE2* into some very rough weather. The P&O cruise vessel *Oriana* had left the States a day previously and had diverted her course to go to the assistance of 76-year old lone sailor, Jack Nye, whose yacht had been dismasted in the prevailing gale. During her rescue mission the *Oriana* suffered structural damage with cabins well above the waterline being severely flooded. Several passengers and members of the crew were injured by glass broken by the 40-foot wave. *QE2* sailed unscathed through the bad weather and arrived in Southampton a day ahead of the P&O ship.

The 2001 World Cruise, billed as the 'Voyage of Great Discoveries', was preceded after her departure from Southampton on November 14th by a cruise to the Caribbean and started in earnest from New York on 5th January, 2001. During the course of the world cruise the liner called into Dubai, a Gulf port that was endeavouring to become a major cruise destination and was planning to build a huge leisure island in the form of a palm tree.

Staying overnight between 25th and 26th March the *QE2* was the principal guest vessel amongst other cruise ships at the opening of the Dubai Cruise Terminal at Port Rashid.

Trouble hit the liner on 26th May shortly after leaving Southampton *en-route* for the Mediterranean. At 2am that night, whilst still in the English Channel, difficulties were experienced with the steering gear and the liner came to a halt, drifting in misty conditions, whilst her engineers worked through the night to rectify the fault. Warnings were sent out to other ships in the area to take extra care but the ship was underway once again before many passengers had awoken. Captain Paul Wright, however, made a broadcast that morning to keep the passengers informed of what had happened.

On an April Atlantic cruise to Madeira and Lisbon from New York shortly after the end of her 2001 world cruise the liner received a distress call when an emergency had arisen on board a Spanish fishing vessel. One of the fishing boat's crewmembers had received a wound to his head so, in response, the Cunarder turned in her tracks and retraced her course for 150 miles, arriving at the scene at around eight in the evening.

The ship's surgeon, Dr Martin Carroll, was taken in one of the *QE2*'s boats and, deciding that the head wound was serious enough, had the fisherman transferred to the waiting liner. As a result the ship missed her scheduled call at Madeira on the 28th April and proceeded straight to Lisbon. The rescued sailor received many cards from both passengers and crew and apparently made a full recovery.

Between the loss of the French airline's Concorde and its sisters' reintroduction into service a greater tragedy occurred, the ramifications of which had - and, at the time of writing, still has - enormous effect on the West and on the industry in which the *QE2* is involved.

On 10th September, 2001, the *QE2* left Southampton at 5pm on one of her scheduled voyages to New York where she was due to arrive early on the morning of the 16th. A fine early summer's evening saw the liner sailing eastwards through The Solent, the still bright evening sun of late summer picking out her size and livery to its best effect.

But, as with her predecessor - the *Queen Mary* - sailing westwards in September of 1939 on the eve of the outbreak of the Second World War, international affairs would take a drastic, unexpectedly tragic and violent turn of events before her journey's end.

On the second day of her voyage the security of the world was changed for ever as three aircraft, loaded with innocent passengers and piloted by Islamic fundamentalist terrorists' hands, slammed with spectacular eruptions of consuming flame, acrid smoke and destruction into American and international confidence. On one of the brightest and clearest days of the year, two of the highjacked aircraft found prime targets in the imposing twin towers of the World Trade Center in the financial heart of New York. The third passenger aircraft was crashed into the nerve centre of US defence in Washington, the Pentagon. A fourth 'plane crashed prevented from reaching its target by heroic passengers who overpowered the terrorists on-board.

'September the Eleventh' subsequently became by-words for infamy and horror.

Those on board the liner shared with the rest of the civilised world feelings that combined horror, shock and a disbelieving fascination as the dreadful spectacle was replayed over on television screens. There was no possible

A sight often seen in the past but one that will never again reoccur - the *QE2*, outward bound, slips by the twin towers of New York's World Trade Centre.   *Cunard*

way that the *Queen Elizabeth 2* could proceed to New York so, as on other occasions in her past, the ship was diverted to Boston. Even her arrival - and that of the similarly diverted *Caronia* - was delayed because telephoned bomb threats caused the closure of the harbour. The two ships were held outside the port whilst their terminal was inspected.

As the smoke still rose from hundreds of thousands of tonnes of rubble that marked the ruins of the twin towers and the graves of the thousands that had died Pier 92, near to the *QE2*'s usual berth at Pier 90 in New York, was occupied in the month that followed the attack by the United States Naval Ship *Comfort* (T-AH 20). This big, white ship with three red crosses painted on each side was used to provide assistance to the search and rescue teams and to provide food and short-term lodging space for firemen and disaster recovery personnel. The cruise terminal used by *Queen Elizabeth 2* was used by the Federal Emergency Management Agency as a command centre and as a departure point for boats transporting bereaved families so that they could view 'Ground Zero' from the river.

The WTC towers had collapsed appallingly quickly and the after-shock of the terrorism that caused their disintegration created a loss of confidence in air and sea travel. Major airlines saw demand for seats plummet and a few companies actually went out of business. Although the severe losses in cruise line share values (Carnival Corporation - Cunard's parent company - had millions wiped off their stock market value) had recovered by 20% by mid-November it was too late for some cruise lines as they suffered a sudden loss of trade. With massive numbers of cancellations due to both 11th September and a general slowdown in the world economy Renaissance Cruises filed for bankruptcy with their ships ceasing operations immediately; the entire fleet being eventually offered for sale. American Classic Voyages' two new 1,900-berth cruise-ships that were being built in the United States (the first to be constructed there for many years) were cancelled whilst only 40% and 55% complete. It was later suggested that the vessels could be completed as troopships.

It would not take long for Carnival's own fortunes to be revived as by mid-January, 2002, the cruise company was reporting record levels of bookings and were planning to operate a 24-hour day booking system.

Other cruise companies were requesting shipyards to slow down on the completion of newbuildings until a hoped-for recovery in demand for berths commenced, but the Cunard (under the guardianship of the Carnival Corporation) did exactly the opposite. Not only were Carnival/Cunard going ahead with their exciting new project but the company actually brought forward the start date of their prestigious new 150,000gt, 345-metre, £538million *Queen Mary 2* at the French yard of Chantiers de l'Atlantique at St. Nazaire.

The first steel for this, the first true liner to be built for decades, was cut at a ceremony attended by the Line's new President and Chief of Operations, Pamela Conover. (The previous President and CEO of Cunard Line Limited, Larry Pimentel, had resigned his position as of February 2001 to become co-owner and CEO of a new cruise line, SunDream Yacht Club). The cut shapes of plate and section will be welded into panels and these panels will, in turn, be formed into blocks (sections of ship). These blocks, previously fitted out with piping, cables, etc, will eventually be erected on the building berth to gradually form the hull of the liner. Amazingly, the entire hull and funnels of the 'old' *Queen Mary* could fit inside the massive hull of her intended

The US Naval ship *Comfort* (T-AH 20) at berth in Pier 92. The *QE2*'s berth 90 is on the far right.
US Navy photo by Cheif Photographer's Mate Eric J. Tilford

namesake, as could almost the whole of the *QE2*!

For the three months following the 11th September attack the *Queen Elizabeth 2* would make Boston her American destination for the three calls that she had been scheduled to make. New York Harbour was effectively closed to external passenger traffic as work on clearing 'Ground Zero' continued and the threat of further terrorist attack was evaluated. The piers along the Hudson were blocked-off by a fleet of barges.

On 12th November, however, the first cruise-ship to call into the port for a month, the new Royal Caribbean Cruise Lines' *Adventure of the Seas* (at 137,300 gross tons she and her sisters were the current largest cruise-ships in the world) arrived on her delivery voyage (without passengers) from her builders. The ship lay alongside Berth 1 at Pier 88 to be named by representatives of the New York Police and Fire Departments (both of which had lost many of their members in the early stages of rescue at 'Ground Zero') and by the City mayor, Rudolph Giuliani, who spoke at the naming ceremony. Mayor Giuliani would later, in February 2002, receive an honourary Knighthood from the hand of HM Queen Elizabeth II for the way in which he had handled the emergency in Manhattan. He received the accolade on behalf of the Police, Firefighters and other heroes of New York.

The newly christened *Adventure of the Seas* then took 2,800 relatives and friends of emergency service employees who had been killed on 11th September on a complimentary two-day cruise. At the cruise's end the officers amongst them were called to duty almost immediately to attend American Airlines flight 587 that had crashed onto the Rockaway Beach area in the Borough of Queens shortly after take-off from JFK Airport. Fearing another terrorist attack the vessel, in the high state of emergency that was declared for the city, was immediately ordered out of the port. She returned the following day (after the crash had proved to be an accident) to pick up those members of her crew stranded by her sudden departure.

After the horrific events of 11th September it may be a respite to recall a few of many amusing incidents that have occurred on board the *Queen Elizabeth 2*. One of the ship's officers recalled an occasion when an elderly lady passenger became trapped in a jammed lift. Using the lift's emergency

An artists impression of the new Cunarder, *Queen Mary 2*. Alonside you can see the first ship of the fleet, the Britannia. *Cunard*

telephone her call was quickly answered by an officer on the Bridge. Eager to effect a quick rescue the officer asked the passenger where she was. The reply came back, 'On a big liner in the middle of the ocean.' Unperturbed, the officer informed the stranded passenger that a rescue team would be with her in five minutes. 'That's very quick as you have so far to come' the lady replied, assuming that the rescue team had to come from the shore!

The imposing figurehead of Britannia that used to grace the original Britannia Restaurant had for some time been placed in the foyer just forward of the Mauretania Restaurant on Upper Deck. A broad band of steel bolted the figurehead to the adjacent bulkhead, but this was not to prevent the old lady from falling over in rough seas but to prevent roguish colleagues from once again removing her to the more comfortable confines of some unsuspecting officer's bed!

The *QE2*'s steering wheel had evoked many comments when the liner had first appeared because of its small diameter. After a visit to the Bridge by a group of school children the wheel was found to be missing. Too late to locate another before sailing the mighty *Queen Elizabeth 2* was navigated safely across the North Atlantic and back using a pair of mole grips in lieu of the missing wheel!

October brought forth at least one happy occasion on board when Captain Warwick had the pleasure of officiating at his daughter's wedding, although it happened in Boston rather than the hoped for location of New York. A special permit was obtained from the office of the Governor of Massachusetts for, as a layman, to perform the ceremony and the happy couple also obtained a rushed-through marriage licence. Since that marriage it has been proposed in Great Britain that laws that have prevented weddings being conducted on board ships had to be reformed, an action that will hopefully encourage more owners of cruiseships to re-register their vessels under the Red Ensign.

From 21st November, 2001, prior to her World Cruise that began on 11th December, the *Queen Elizabeth 2* underwent her annual refit, again undertaken at the Bremerhaven yard of Lloyd Werft.

At a reported £19.5m the work carried out included refurbishment of the two Grand Suites. A total revamp of the uninspiring work that had been previously carried out in the Queen's Grill and adjoining Lounge included the addition of a decorative glass-reinforced gypsum frieze contained within an alcove complete with oil gilded lattice work, all being illuminated by concealed lighting. The restaurant's columns were encased in sycamore, ebony and maple burr veneered panelling. Similar panels were fitted to the window surrounds in the Grill Lounge showing off the new curtains. Furniture in both rooms was also reupholstered. New, specially designed chandeliers were also fitted.

The Yacht Club was redecorated, furniture reupholstered and carpets renewed with new joinery work enhancing windows, etc, as in the restaurant area.

After starting her 2001/2002 World Cruise, 'Voyage of Exploration' (from Southampton to Southampton in 127 Nights' from 11th December) the *Queen Elizabeth 2* arrived at New York on 7th January after her usual preliminary cruise to the Atlantic and Caribbean Isles. On her arrival in the Hudson, the first major passenger liner to enter the port on a scheduled cruise since the destruction of the twin towers, the *Queen Elizabeth 2* made a ceremonial stop opposite 'Ground Zero'. Beautifully and impressively illuminated by her on-board lights in the semi-darkness of early morning a moment of remembrance of the events of 11th September was held. The liner, surrounded by the lyricism of the whispering ocean, lowered the Stars and Stripes to half-mast and a wreath gently dropped over the side into the river.

After transiting the Panama Canal a traditional call into Honolulu preceded the vessel's progression across the Pacific which introduced a change from other world cruises when a call into Fiji was omitted.

This stemmed from 19th May 2000 when a group of dissatisfied indigenous islanders, led by George Speight, removed the then Prime Minister (of Indian extraction of the Fijiian island of Suva) from power and held forty two island

Members of Parliament hostage. The prevailing political problems continued for some time with a resultant negative effect on tourism. The *Queen*'s itinerary was subsequently altered on this current cruise calling instead into Papeete, the Tahitian capital, and the nearby island of Moorea.

At the time of writing it has been announced that Cunard has expressed an interest in building yet another new ship. This newbuilding, to be constructed in Italy, will be around the 85,000 gross tonnes mark - similar to the long-held record of the tonnage of the old *Queen Elizabeth*! It also seems likely that the *QE2* will now make only one transatlantic round voyage in conjunction with the new *QM2* in 2003, thus providing an unique opportunity to re-enact the times when the *Queen Mary* and *Queen Elizabeth* used to spectacularly pass each other in mid-Atlantic within a mile of each other. Stephen Payne, Carnival Corporation's chief Naval Architect, can not as yet decide whether to be onboard the *QE2* to see his latest ship in mid-Atlantic or to be on board the *QM2* to see his old favourite from her successor! The *QE2*, then relinquishing her epithet of 'The Last Great Ocean Liner', will then be transferred to full-time cruising whilst 'exploring new liner markets', perhaps being retained in this role for another ten years!

The sistership mooted for the 150,000gt *Queen Mary 2* (the first true liner to be built for almost three decades and under construction at the French shipyard of Chantiers de l'Atlantique, the yard that had built the beautiful *Normandie* - the arch-rival to the old *Queen Mary*) may bear the name *Queen Victoria*, a name originally envisaged by Cunard for the first *Queen Mary*. A suggestion has also been put forward that, on her 'retirement', the *Queen Elizabeth 2* could possibly join the venerable old *Queen Mary* in her retirement at Long Beach near to the proposed Carnival Cruise Terminal that is planned for the area. An idea put forward by a business consortium in Southampton to use the *Queen Mary* as a hotel for passengers embarking on the *Queen Elizabeth 2* had the bid for the Long Beach based liner not been thwarted by her withdrawal from sale in 1991 will now become a reality in California.

In November 2001 it was announced that P&O Princess Cruises and Royal Caribbean Cruises Limited were planning an amalgamation of interests thus forming the world's largest cruise line, thereby taking that distinction away from the Carnival Corporation.

Towards the end of December Carnival entered the fray and expressed their intention to make a hostile bid for P&O Princess Cruises and over the ensuing weeks would four times increase their offer to over £5 billion.

The ensuing 'battle' has produced some startling proposals, not least was the indication that Carnival would be willing to appease European legislation by relinquishing their European holdings. This would mean disposing of Holland-America and their prestigious new acquisition - the Cunard!

So, at the time of writing, the future of the Cunard Line and its ships seems uncertain. A question mark would also seem to hover over the future of the biggest passenger liner ever to be built - what will become of the *Queen Mary* Project?

The last chapter for the *Queen Elizabeth 2* has obviously yet to be written. By the time that this comes to fruition the 'New Cunarder' will undoubtedly have travelled many more thousands of miles, bringing pleasure to untold numbers of people, both on board or wistfully watching her from a distance.

May the *QE2* continue to enjoy (hopefully, in spite of the current uncertainties) that which Her Majesty Queen Elizabeth II wished the ship during her launching speech on 20th September, 1967:

'A long life and good fortune'.

Whether sailing through the vagaries of Nature or Accountancy, the *Queen Elizabeth 2* more often than not reaches a safe haven on a tide of good management, great care and goodwill.
Cunard

Acknowledgements

In this necessarily brief but updated account of the career of the *Queen Elizabeth 2* I have tried to paint a broad picture, highlighting some events whilst briefly touching on others. I apologise if I have missed out any particularly favourite story about the ship but space, of course, precluded the inclusion of everything! The *Queen* still continues with an amazingly action-packed career and, for some of the headline stories of her thirty years of sailing the oceans of the world, I have endeavoured to obtain first-hand accounts of some of those particular incidents. For these I am particularly grateful to: Cunard's Public Relations Department (notably Eric Flounders and Michael Gallagher); Boyd Haining (ex-Shipyard Manager at John Browns, Shipbuilders and Engineers); Captain Peter Jackson; Captain (then First Officer) Philip Rentell; and last, but in no means least, Captain Robin Woodall not only for his wonderful recollections but for his patient reading of the manuscript, for contributing an excellent Foreword and for suggesting corrections to the original book.

Cunard's shore staff of two continents should also be mentioned. Theirs is a job which goes largely unsung but without them, between the enormous organisation that culminates in the endless stream of brochures that initiate many voyages and the final offloading of baggage at the end of a voyage, the QE2 would not be run so efficiently. Amongst the many others whom I would wish to thank are the authors of many invaluable most informative books including; Messrs. Potter and Frost; Captain Ron Warwick; my good and knowledgeable friend, William H Miller and his co-author Luis Miguel Correia; and Gary C Buchanan whose own book wonderfully captures in photographs the many changes that have occurred to the QE2 over the years.

In addition to the above I would like to express my appreciation (posthumously , I regret to say, in the cases of a few since the appearance of the first edition) to the following people and their respective organisations for either their time and patience during my interrogations or for loaning precious photographs or artefacts: Fabian Acker ("Motor Ship"); Wally Adams; Nigel Allan; June Appleby; Brian Atkinson; Mr. Ballard (GEC Electrical Projects Ltd.,); Bob Bantock; Len Betts; John T. Brown; Wyn Coombe; Robert Cove; Department of the Navy (US), Frank B. Randall jnr; Captain Ian Dunderdale (Cromarty Forth Port Authority); Audrey and Steve Dymock: Richard Faber (Ocean Liner Memorabilia of 230 East 15thSt., NY, NY10003); Michael A. Findlay; Barney Gallagher; George Gardner; Lilian Gibson: Bob Bruce Grice; Les and Thomas Gough; Charles Haas; Jenny Haining; John Havers; Imperial War Museum, London; Norman Jackman; Marvin Jensen; Tim Jone; Diana Johnston (of MaGregor-Navire Publications Ltd.,); P. A. Kroehenst; Katherine Leiper (daughter of John Rannie); Terry Little; Liverpool University; Staff Captain Ian MacNaught; Commodore Geoffrey Marr; Gordon Matthews (GEC Turbines Ltd.,); William H. Miller; Peter Newall; Nigel Overton; Royal Torbay Yacht Club; Scottish Records Office; Peter Seden (for his wonderful additional photographs of the liner's 1999 interiors); Southampton Central Library; Southampton Maritime Museum; Southampton Daily Echo (especially Peter Ashton and Keith Hamilton); Liz Stephens; "Titanic" International (PO Box 7007, Freehold, NJ 7728-7007, USA); University of Glasgow Business Archives; Cedric Wasser; John Watson (MAN-B&W Diesels Ltd.,) and Peter Weiss.

My publisher, Roger Hardingham, I thank for his perseverance after requesting three additional chapters to update my original book but received 30,000 words in return!

Bibliography

Arnott, Captain Robert, Captain of the Queen (New English Library, 1982).

Bonsor, N.R.P., North Atlantic Seaway, Vol. 1 (David & Charles, 1975).

Buchanan, Gary C., Queen Elizabeth 2 - A Magnificent Millennium (Past and present Publishing Ltd., 1996).

Cunard Line, The Cunarders 1840-1969 (Peter Barker Publishing Ltd.,); - Pleasure Island (1969?); - Sailing Into a Great Tradition (1982 souvenir World Cruise book).

Hutchings, David F., RMS Queen Mary - 50 Years of Splendour (Kingfisher Railway Productions, Southampton, 1986).

Hutchings, David F., Caronia - Legacy of a Pretty Sister (Shipping Books Press, 2000).

Hyde, Frances E., Cunard and the North Atlantic (The MacMillan Press Ltd., 1975).

Johnson, Howard, The Cunard Story (Whittet Books, 1987).

Kludas, Arnold, Passenger Ships of the World, Vol. 5, 1951-1976 (Patrick Stephens, Cambridge, 1977).

Lloyd Werft, Bremerhaven, Queen Elizabeth 2 - The History of a Conversion.

Marine Accident Investigation Branch, Report of the Investigation Into the Grounding of Passenger Vessel Queen Elizabeth 2 on 7 August 1992 (HMSO, The Department of Transport, 1993).

Marine Safety Agency, Queen Elizabeth 2 - Voyage From Southampton to New York, December 1994 (MSA, The Department of Transport, Southampton, 1995).

Marr, Commodore Geoffrey T., The Queens and I (Adlard Coles, 19730.

Maxtone Graham, John, Tribute to a Queen (Berlitz Publications, 1987).

Miller, William H., Great Cruise Ships and Ocean Liners from 1954 to 1986(Dover, 1988).

Miller, William H., Transatlantic Liners 1945-1980 (David & Charles, 1984).

Miller, William H. and Correia, Luis Miguel, RMS Queen Elizabeth 2 of 1969 (Liner Books, Lisbon, 1999).

Miller, William H. and Hutchings, David F., Transatlantic Liners at War - The Story of the Queens ((David & Charles, 1985).

National Transportation Safety Board, Grounding of the United Kingdom Passenger Vessel RMS Queen Elizabeth 2 Near Cuttyhunk Island, Vineyard sound, Massachusetts, August 7, 1992 (NTSB, Washington DC 20594, USA).

Potter, Neil and Frost, Jack, Queen Elizabeth 2 - The Authorised Story (Harrap, 1969).

Ransome-Wallis, P., North Atlantic Panorama 1900-1976 (Ian Allan, 1977).

Rentell, Philip, Historic Cunard Liners (Atlantic, 1986).

Roberts, Dr. Nigel, C-Six - Ten Years as the Doctor of the QE2 (Sidgwick & Jackson, 1988).

Southampton Corporation, The Queens (Harvey Barton-St. Stephens Publication, 1969).

Taylor, Arthur, Great Liners (Southern Newspapers, Southampton).

Villar, Captain Roger, Merchant Ships at War Conway/Lloyds of London Press, 1984).

Wall, Robert, Ocean Liners (Collins, 1978).

Warwick, Captain Ronald, QE2 (W.W. Norton & Company, revised edition 1998). **Newspapers** Daily Telegraph; Lloyds List, Portsmouth News; The Times; Southampton Daily Echo. **Journals and Periodicals** Bremerhaven Magazine No. 79, Mai/April 1987; CME (Journal of Chartrered Mechanical Engineers) May 1987; Cruise Digest reports, Vol 6 Special Issue No. 1, 1987; Cunard publicity brochures, Press Releases, etc.; Diesel and Gas Turbine Worldwide Engineering, 13 December, 1968; 100A1 (Journal of Lloyds Register of Shipping) July 1986; Lloyds Ship Manager, May 1987; ME/LOG, August 1986; MacGregor-Navire News, April 1986; Marine Propulsion, Special Issue Rebirth of a Queen, May 1987; MPS Review, September 1986;; The Motor Ship, June 1987; The Naval Architect (Journal of the Institution of Naval Architects), various dates; Sea Breezes; Sea Lines (journal of the Ocean Liner Society, 27 Old Gloucester St., London); Ships Monthly; Shipbuilding and Shipping Record, various but especially Supplement of 31 January, 1969; Shipping World and Shipbuilder; Shipping - Today and Yesterday.

The Sir Oswald Birley portrait of HM The Queen Mother, as she was when Queen Elizabeth, that originally hung on the *Queen Elizabeth*.

Peter Seden

HM Queen Elizabeth The Queen Mother
1900 - 2002

Sir John Brown
1901 - 2000